DISENCHANTED CITY

La ville désenchantée

CHANTAL BIZZINI

Edited by Marilyn Kallet and J. Bradford Anderson
Translated by J. Bradford Anderson, Darren Jackson,
and Marilyn Kallet

DISENCHANTED CITY

La ville désenchantée

CHANTAL BIZZINI

Edited by Marilyn Kallet and J. Bradford Anderson
Translated by J. Bradford Anderson, Darren Jackson,
and Marilyn Kallet

Joseph S. Phillips and Susan J. Wood, Ph.D., Publishers
www.blackwidowpress.com

Design & production: Kerrie Kemperman
Cover image: « Petit matin à Barbès » by Chantal Bizzini

ISBN: 978-0-9960079-6-2
Printed in the United States

10 9 8 7 6 5 4 3 2 1

« C'est donc toi, cruel argent, qui sèmes d'inquiétudes la vie humaine, et nous ouvres avant le temps le chemin du trépas ! Tu es le funeste aliment de nos vices, le germe de nos soucis. »[1]

"You, therefore, cruel money, sow troubles throughout human life, and open before our time the path of death! It's you that gives men's vices deadly nourishment, the seed of our woes."

Propertius, Lib. iii, *Elegies,* vii (1–4)

---

[1] Traduction de J. Genouille (1862).

ACKNOWLEDGEMENTS

Some of the following poems by Chantal Bizzini have been previously published in Europe and in the United States; several of these have been accompanied by translations. Gratefully we acknowledge the following journals and their editors:

"Saint Sébastien," "Tombeau du Printemps," "Éclat métallique," *Le Mâche-Laurier*

"Tombeau du Printemps," "Ida, en miroir" "Au moment de mourir," "Un fruit étrange," *Action Poétique*

"Tombeau du Printemps," "Ida, en miroir," "Nos jeux traversés, "La chasse," *Backwoods Broadsides,* with translations by J. Bradford Anderson ("Ida in the Mirror," "Our Interrupted Games," "The Hunt")

"Ida, en miroir," "Carte postale," "Le Dauphin," *Rehauts*

"Carte postale," "Éclat métallique," "Célébration," *Public Republic,* with translations by Marilyn Kallet ("Postcard," "Metallic Flash," "Celebration")

"Jazz," excerpt from "La Tour Lumière," *mouvances*

"Nos oiseaux," "Translation," "La chasse," *Poésie 2001*

"La coupe obscure," *Mixitini Matrix,* with translation by Marilyn Kallet ("The Dark Cup")

"La Tour Lumière," *Luvina foros,* with translation by Silvia E. Castillero ("La Torre Luz")

"Le Club 55," *Poezibao*

"Louxor, Palais du cinéma," *Europe* and in *Two Lines: World Writing in Translation,* with translation by J. Bradford Anderson ("Luxor, Movie Palace")

"Louxor, Palais du cinéma," online at *Les Amis du Louxor*

"Une journée, ici," *Siècle 21*

"Tombeau du Printemps," "Nos oiseaux," "Éclat métallique," "Louxor, Palais du cinéma," "Énigme," "Translation," "Travestissements," *Vakxikon*. Translated into Greek by Angeliki Dimouli.

Additional translations by J. Bradford Anderson: "The Disenchanted City," "Into the Night," "September," "Birds," *Esopus Magazine*.

Acknowledgements from J. Bradford Anderson:
I am indebted to the late Sylvester Pollet for bringing Bizzini's poetry into English for the first time in his *Backwoods Broadsides* series. I am thankful to Zack Rogow for publishing Bizzini in *Two Lines,* an extraordinary journal of translation that brought me into contact with Marilyn Kallet. How lucky I've been! Lucky, too, for working with another fine poet, Darren Jackson, on these translations. Tod Lippy provided a gorgeous home—a whole atmosphere, really—for Bizzini's poetry in *Esopus Magazine*.

Acknowledgements from Darren Jackson:
Thanks to Chantal, Brad, and Marilyn for comments on several drafts of the translations. Whatever felicity these translations bear is due to their insight.

Acknowledgements from Marilyn Kallet:
Thanks to J. Bradford Anderson, who introduced me to Chantal and her work. Chantal has been tireless in helping us translate this work accurately and with lyrical verve. She has also shown me the best bistros in Paris, one of which is at her house. Best apricot tart! We have walked the streets of Paris together, and so I have been steeped in the atmosphere of this book, this volume of fragments and shores, of Light Towers and artsy cinemas, luxury and poverty, the mélange that is contemporary Paris. Her *Disenchanted City* offers collages of Paris in words. My co-translators, J. Bradford Anderson and Darren Jackson,

are the dream team for translation. And speaking of superb poet-translators, Marilyn Hacker has offered steady encouragement. There's no one like her for talent and generosity.

Leslie LaChance at *Mixitini Matrix* and Katerina Stoykova-Klemer at *Public Republic* have welcomed Chantal's work and our translations.

Joe Phillips at Black Widow Press continues to create a home for poetry in translation, especially for translations from the French. His hospitality gives shelter to some of the best modern and contemporary poetry, among them the wild-eyed Surrealists.

The University of Tennessee Department of English and the Graduate School Professional Development fund have supported my research, writing, and translation in France for almost a decade. Production of this book was supported by the department, the College of Arts & Sciences, and the university's Exhibit, Performance, and Publication Expenses Fund. I will always be grateful.

Kerrie Kemperman and Angie Biggs helped to edit this manuscript in various stages. Their eyes caught the glitches so that the readers' eyes would be spared! Blessed are copy editors, for their work is invisible.

TABLE OF CONTENTS

IV

V

IN THIS SEASON
En cette saison

THE LIGHT TOWER
La Tour Lumière

PREFACE

J. Bradford Anderson

When I was living in Paris I used to meet Chantal Bizzini in her eighteenth arrondissement walk-up for three hours a week to discuss nineteenth- and twentieth-century literature. She returned my compositions covered in ink, red for grammar mistakes, green for errors in argument. She was exhaustively prepared for each of our sessions, referring to extensive notes and, more impressively, her memory, which seemed to range over most of nineteenth- and twentieth-century French literature. About halfway through our sessions, she asked if I wanted to take a break; inevitably, I did. She retired to the kitchen and brought back tea and snacks, and then she put on some Fauré, Debussy, or whoever would serve as good accompaniment to the author of the week. We chatted a bit, and she would suggest small museums to see, walks to take, movies to view. Then, fifteen or twenty minutes later she would put away the tea things and we went back to work.

Many years later I realized that those breaks were a kind of lesson, revealing that the line between the literature I was studying and the life I was leading was permeable, perhaps illusory.

After our last tutorial, she asked if I wanted to take a walk. We made our way up a hill to Nerval's home, a dilapidated, ivy-colored haunted house. We resumed that journey two years later when she came to California, my home at the time. As we crossed a narrow ribbon of bridge over what seemed a huge chasm in the growing dark, I recited these lines from Nerval's "El Desdichado": "Et j'ai deux fois vainqueur traversé l'Achéron" ("And I crossed the Acheron twice victorious"). To which Bizzini replied, "Modulant tour à tour sur la lyre d'Orphée / Les soupirs de la Sainte et les cris de la Fée" ("Modulating on Orpheus' lyre each in its turn / The sighs of the Saint and the cries of the Fairy"). Together we had recited the final tercet of Nerval's "El Desdichado." Literature crossed with life.

From Bizzini I learned that to be a poet is to be in motion, to leave the study for the kitchen (and then come back), leave the apartment for Nerval's house, leave France for California, and cross the line between work and world. Guy Debord's Situationist manifesto, *Society of the Spectacle,* provides one possible context for Bizzini's work. Her poems often begin in the Debordian *dérive,* the active though unplanned exploration of urban topography. Many of Bizzini's poems range over the neglected terrain of Paris and its *banlieue:* "Luxor, Movie Palace," for instance, or "Le Dauphin." Others begin further afield. Part of "A Strange Fruit," for example, takes place in the American South. Many of her poems, however, layer several journeys in collage-like patterns, so "A Strange Fruit" makes its way to Seville and "September" links the World Trade Center to Bizzini's own neighborhood. The vertiginous layering of multiple trajectories displaces attention from the physical *dérive* to a kind of mental odyssey, and suggests other literary contexts. The Surrealists, with their deliberate short-circuiting of logic and love of collage effects, are predecessors. And yet Bizzini never departs entirely from the material and subjective facts of her actual journeys, and her syntax, however complex, never entirely abandons meaning for the free play of the signifier. Our challenge, then, is to make some kind of provisional sense out of the juxtapositions of place and time, fact and myth.

The key word is "provisional," because Bizzini is uninterested in repopulating the urban environment with resonant symbols. Like the narrator of Baudelaire's "Le Cygne," she shares

the lament that "la forme d'une ville / Change plus vite, hélas !
que le cœur d'un mortel" ("the form of a city / Changes faster,
alas, than the heart of a mortal"). Besides, she is moving too fast.
As she hurtles along the elevated railway in "Luxor," she moves:

> beyond maps
> …we pass
> in front of walled-
> up buildings, broken, crumbling,
> collapsed where the construction site that knocks down,
> eviscerates, shows
> what facades still hide: these islands
> with the fountain and the tree,
> anachronistic refuge and repose,
> the lean-tos with low roofs,
> the diseased life, squatters, blind buildings,
> the leprous and gated roads
> where I have heard that children sell themselves.

But we are not in "The Waste Land." Bizzini refuses to hang a
Golden Bough over "the fountain and the tree." The train is
going too fast and she has a responsibility to notice the squatters,
the broken roads, the prostitutes, all the ruined dependencies of
this insufficient "refuge and repose," this inadequate symbolic
landscape.

Despite Bizzini's flight from reified knowledge in favor of a
provisional personal vision, she is uninterested in magnifying the
lyric self. She avoids the first person singular, although she will
occasionally deploy an unidentifiable first person plural. She
comes closest to self-disclosure towards the end of "Le Dauphin"
when a strange figure enters Bizzini's world of stupefied com-
muters, thugs and lonely men: *l'écrivain public* ("the public
writer"). Because Bizzini has translated a number of Adrienne

Rich's poems into French and has written extensively on Ezra Pound, I tend to see her "public writer" in the company of these politically divergent American poets who nevertheless all tried to "contain" (to borrow Pound's verb) history in poetry by abandoning strictly lyric modes for a more "public" voice. Bizzini is the poet of the new France: the France of burning cars and alienated immigrants, of underemployment and boredom, of hatred and "*précarité.*"

Take "Dauphin," for instance, a term rich in royalist associations. In Bizzini's France, "Le Dauphin" turns out to be an all night dive brimming with marginal people who have been rendered invisible as Paris transforms itself into a museum of itself, Venice on the Seine. "Luxor," a name evoking Napoléon's march into Egypt, Champollion and his hieroglyphs—in brief, the nineteenth-century Orientalist project—turns out to be a ruined movie theatre, a Platonic cave (think of the "multitudes bent toward some flashing scene / Never disclosed" in Hart Crane's *The Bridge*) where all the fires have gone out. The public writer in motion takes us well beyond the reified mythologies of the nineteenth-century Orientalists and introduces us instead to child prostitutes, probably Arab: "The coal of their eyes, / The mint of their breath." The reader moves "beyond" the official, falsifying maps (Adrienne Rich's "book of myths in which our names do not appear").

The collection opens with images of death—Gaudier-Brzeska's (that Poundian inheritance), Saint Sebastian's, Villon's, Billie Holiday's, the Spanish anarchists'—and makes its way not to a kind of rebirth but to a kind of meaningful persistence, plausible endurance. *Disenchanted City* closes with the sequence "The Light Tower," which evokes a utopian architecture, a surer repository of remembrance than our frail bodies, a potentially dignified backdrop for our brief lives:

— Listen to the ductile air,
sparkling with fabrics,
this Sunday, when groups
of West African women
stroll down the streets like this
celebrating this day.

The Luxor itself has undergone the kind of movement towards architectural rebirth sketched in Bizzini's work. It was reinvented first as a Caribbean dance club, then as one of the hottest gay clubs in Paris and now, once more, as a gorgeous cinema, a true tower of light.

Bizzini has moved from institutional knowledge to poetic vision in her own life. She was born in 1956 and has lived most of her life in Paris. After first studying to become a curator, she obtained a Ph.D. in Comparative Literature from the University of Paris, writing on the persistence of antiquity in the poetry of Ezra Pound and Hart Crane. Bizzini began publishing poetry in the early eighties and has published translations of English and American poets, including Ezra Pound, Hart Crane, W. H. Auden, Adrienne Rich, Denise Levertov, John Ashbery, Clayton Eshleman, Henri Cole, and Jorie Graham in *Po&sie, Europe, Poésie 2005, Action Poétique, Le Mâche-Laurier, Rehauts,* and *Siècle 21.* Bizzini has also translated from Italian and Portuguese. Her poems have been translated and published in Italy, Spain, Mexico, Canada, and Greece. She is also a visual artist, creating complex collages of urban landscapes with photographs and digitally manipulated images, analogues of her complex, palimpsestic poems.

INTRODUCTION

Marilyn Kallet

Male poet, male poet, male poet. As I perused the shelves in Paris bookstores looking for French women poets to translate, I found myself more and more frustrated. In Librairie Dédale, amid shelves of male writers in the Gallimard editions, I did locate two women: Sylvia Plath and Emily Dickinson. In French.

So when I came across Chantal Bizzini's poem, "Luxor," in *Two Lines: World Writing in Translation,* I was thrilled. Not just because I had found a contemporary Parisian woman poet, but because her poetry was bubbling with imaginative play, heady like Apollinaire's *Alcools,* dazzling both in French and in the English translation. Everything seemed to be happening at once in this poetry: street scenes came to life, architectural outlines, streets and alleyways were mapped, illumined; notes on the quality of light became an essential part of the composition. In a single poem we sampled a slice of the history, art, and social life of the eighteenth arrondissement. Alongside classical grandeur, Egyptian Art Deco raised its gold-embossed head; next to new construction grew decay; bustling streets near the theater held poverty and child sexual slavery. I would never argue that this poem was pretty. But yes, Emily, it did take off the top of my head. Chantal's corner of Paris in "Luxor" offered a vibrant, sonorous landscape, "marked by strange signals from a country / beyond maps." That's the country of poetry, and in that buzzing atmosphere of a city-hive, I tasted honey. Brad Anderson's translation was damned good, as lyrical and lively as the original French. That's not a translation, my friends, it's a miracle!

Quickly I wrote to J. Bradford Anderson and asked him about Chantal Bizzini. Within a few weeks I heard back from him with Chantal's contact information, and my correspondence with both Chantal and Brad came to life. I will always be grateful to Brad for this personal introduction to Chantal. Sometimes translators act as if they own the author they are translating. Brad has written to me, on the contrary, that his only goal is to see that Chantal's poetry is made available to the reading public.

In 2009, my husband Lou Gross and I visited Chantal Bizzini and her husband Frédéric at their apartment in the bustling eighteenth arrondissement. Chantal and I spoke easily of our literary loves; foremost among them was Adrienne Rich, whose poetry Chantal had translated. Others she had grappled with included some of our most difficult poets, Hart Crane, Ezra Pound, Clayton Eshleman, and Jorie Graham. Fred spoke of his love of jazz, a subject he has taught at l'Université de Paris 8 in music history classes. Chantal baked an apricot tart to top all previously tasted tarts, and our friendship was sealed. Before parting, Chantal took us on a walk past the house where Tristan Tzara had lived for a time.

The advantages of translating a living poet cannot be underestimated. Chantal has asked pertinent questions and has made invaluable suggestions and corrections on all of my versions. Éluard and Péret, whose work I have also translated, were not able to be as interactive, alas!

Since 2009 I have met Chantal every spring in Paris, where we have visited historic landmarks and dined together at authentic spots known for regional specialties. I soon learned that Chantal is one of the great contemporary *flâneurs*—she has mapped out every corner of Paris, every good bookstore and bistro and the best pâtisseries. Like Baudelaire, Léon-Paul Fargue, and Apollinaire, Chantal has destroyed more than one pair of shoes strolling through her beloved city. For many years she has tutored for Stanford University, offering independent studies in memoir. I imagine she has taken those lucky students into corners of Paris that tourists rarely know.

Chantal's poems translate busy street life and an intimate knowledge of the city into lyrical shapes. *Disenchanted City* offers a complex environment with seedy sides and crumbling walls, worldly as well as sacred spaces, where Saint Sebastian seems to breathe in the wooden statues of Breton country chapels and in El Greco's paintings. Chantal's educational background focused equally on classical literature and contemporary letters, she took degrees at the Sorbonne as well as École des hautes études en sciences sociales. Recently she has been immersed in the study of modern Greek, which must come in handy during the student tours she leads in Greece. Poems with shorelines and beaches, such as "Ouistreham or Cythera" and "Panorama," reflect Chantal's travels to Greece and Italy, as well as to New York. Indeed "fragmented shores" of modern life are a hallmark of Chantal's poetry; waffles and cotton candy remind us of the commercialization of the beaches; "narrow gardens," rose bushes and earthenware tiles suggest that treasure can still be unearthed by those with an eye for layers, crevices, doorways, and flea markets.

My favorite poems of Chantal's offer portraits of Parisian blues clubs, lyrical poems such as "Le Dauphin," "Carte postale," and "Ida, en miroir." When I asked Chantal about her literary influences, she mentioned not only literary figures—among them Verlaine, Jacques Réda, Adrienne Rich, Hart Crane, Dos Passos, Pound, and Auden—but also jazz greats like Eric Dolphy, Paul Bley, and Emmanuel Bex. She has been strongly influenced by architects, painters, and sculptors, including Nicolas Schöffer and Henri Gaudier-Brzeska, referred to in the first poem of this collection; by Gérard Garouste, painter, decorator, and social activist, and by El Greco, among many others. Photographers and cinematographers have influenced Chantal's work, too; the film influence comes as no surprise, considering the dynamism of her poetry.

Chantal herself is a brilliant photographer and collagist and has been featured in several successful shows in Paris. Her eye for detail and her tenderness toward Paris come through in her photographs as in the poems, where the reader finds bread crumbs on the corner bench, and fragments of marketplace conversation. Collage, and the artistic techniques that we recognize as one hallmark of Modernism, is alive and well in Chantal's work in all its guises. In his Preface, J. Bradford Anderson has remarked that for all its fragments and contradictions this is not "The Waste Land." Agreed. "The Waste Land" never held this much personal warmth.

During our recent Paris meetings to discuss poetry and translation, Chantal and I have included other poets, among them Darren Jackson, who has adeptly translated Michaux, and now beautifully, Chantal Bizzini; we have also met with Marilyn Hacker, one of our greatest living poets and translators of the French. For several years now Hacker has resided in Paris. When I complained to her about the lack of women poets published by mainstream French presses, she dismissed my theory of sexism: "It's poetry they ignore, not just women."

Last spring in Paris I stopped in again at Dédale on rue des Écoles. Their terrific assortment of books by and about Rimbaud took up showcases, windows, and shelves. The contemporary poetry section, mostly Gallimard, was still comprised of over 90 per cent male authors. "Where are the contemporary French women poets?" I asked the woman at the front desk. "They are not writing," she said. I responded, "You're wrong!" I said, "I'm currently translating the poetry of a terrific Parisian poet, Chantal Bizzini." Graciously she said she would be delighted to see the volume once it came out. I plan to hand-deliver *Disenchanted*

City to her and to the wonderful women managers at Librairie Compagnie nearer the Sorbonne; I've only recently discovered their substantial poetry selection.

2015 will be a banner year for Chantal Bizzini's poetry, when *Disenchanted City* makes its American and French debut, and an artist's book of poetry, *Boulevard Magenta*, is published in France by le bousquet-la barthe éditions.

As an editor, I would have chosen to place the jazz/blues poems in the front of this collection. We Americans like to ease our way into the more difficult subjects, and the blues help us with difficult emotional journeys. Chantal would have none of that. She told me she had composed the first few poems in memory of a dear friend of hers who died of AIDS. Those poems had to take the place of honor. When I said I'd prefer to introduce the American reader to her poetry with a little less death, Chantal rattled off a list of French poets and novelists who start with it. "What about Camus? And Gide? What about Yves Bonnefoy? "They're French," I said.

Stubbornness is at least one part of genius, no doubt. Think of Sharon Olds, who was criticized for writing too many poems about her father's death, and who went ahead and composed a whole brilliant book—*The Father*—on the topic. Chantal's poems about her friend's death remind me more specifically of Marie Howe's poetry about her brother's illness and death from AIDS, in *What The Living Do*. And Chantal's poetry holds kinship with Brenda Hillman's work; both poets write about the social and political world with care, tenderness, and anger, as well as about the invisible world of feelings and spirits, the visionary world that grasps moods and intentions beneath surfaces. Chantal Bizzini does not shy away from difficult subjects or from gnostic lyrics that speak to the mind the way music does, without explanation. "O Taste and See," Denise Levertov wrote, using the psalm as her starting point for both engagement with the world and for rebellion against orthodoxy. "The world is not with us enough," Levertov insisted. In Chantal Bizzini's poems the world is with us more, in images summoning art, music, architecture, geography, and marketplaces.

If you can't afford to fly to Paris, you can at least stroll with Chantal in these brilliant, artfully lit poems. But if you do go, carry this volume with you for company and courage. Show it to bookshop owners, to other poets and readers who adore Rimbaud but also crave lyrics in a different voice.

RIVAGE FRAGMENTÉ

FRAGMENTED SHORE

I

SAINT SÉBASTIEN

Vent,
yeux agrandis,
feuilles,
flammèches dans la lumière soudaine,
annoncée par la torsion des branches,
leur craquement,
— les franges de la forêt sont perdues —
la nuit prend, vivifiée,
dans le feu.

Sous ce vent, ce feu,
les murs d'Orléans s'écartent :
tonnerre des fûts qu'on roule dans les rues.
Gaudier devant sa mort :
                    il chancelle dans l'embrasure,
ses bras retombant,
vagues, puis entravés.
La croix.

Une avancée de béton sur l'estuaire,
entaillée, rouillée des coulées de son armature.
Un voilier entre dans le silence ancien
où l'inconnu
heurte l'heure humaine, irisée ;
il va, sans souci
de l'éclosion qui se fait au ciel.

Soleil, corrosion des amarres,
des filins, des mâts,
rouille des ponts volants,
le fer des hangars,

SAINT SEBASTIAN

Wind,
eyes wide,
leaves,
flying sparks in the sudden light,
heralded by the twisting of branches,
their snapping
—the forest's edge is lost—
the night, aroused, catches
fire.

Out of this wind, this fire,
the walls of Orléans open:
thunder of wine vats rolling through the streets.
Gaudier before his death:
                  he staggers in a doorway,
his arms fall,
flail, then are bound.
The cross.

The cement overhanging the estuary,
gashed, rusted from the scaffolding's run-off.
A sail enters into an old silence
where the unknown
hollows the human hour, iridescent;
it floats, oblivious
to the opening sky.

Sun, corroded moorings,
ropes, masts,
rust on the drawbridges,
the iron of boathouses,

les voiles, les oiseaux
touchés ;
écailles des flaques
sur les quais,
les rigoles lâchant
leurs eaux dans les graviers goudronnés.
Lorient,
où cette saison fut déportée,
ville aux avenues larges qui mènent
à la digue d'acier de la mer pourrissante.
Ville désertée
dans les longs sifflements.

Le corps percé,
à l'ombre ;
le vitrail teint de son sang et de son or
le regard
venu trop au bord où se fait un grand jour ;

car aucune barrière n'arrête le
regard levé vers celui qui donne la grâce,
Il se penche : le suppliant, comme plongé dans le feu, acquiert
immédiatement l'éclat.

Parmi les choses muettes,
le corps de celui qui
va se baigner
se retire du monde ;
l'ombre enferme ses membres
et c'est maintenant le crissement du deuil,
les cendres,
les paumes impossibles

sails, the birds
touched;
ragged pools
on the wharfs,
drainage pipes release
their water onto the tar.
Lorient,
where this season was deported,
city of large avenues that lead
to the rotting ocean's iron dike.
Deserted city
in the howling wind.

The pierced body,
in shadow;
the stained-glass window dyed in its blood and in its gold
the gaze
inching too close to the edge of the blazing day;

for no barrier will stop the
look turned to the bestower of grace,
he stoops: the supplicant, as if bathed in fire, immediately
    takes on
the brilliance.

Among mute things,
the body of he who
is going to bathe
retires from the world;
shadow encloses his body
and now the cacophony of mourning,
the ashes,
palms impossible

à joindre,
les yeux sans jour
que tout reflet changeant
a quittés.

(Saint Sébastien
percé de trop de plaies)
À genoux
sur l'herbe fine et lustrée,
quand la terre ici disparaît,
large tache sur les yeux,
sur la langue
— le goût varié
des fruits noirs est perdu ;
les épines,
les feuilles
et les pas
recouverts
peu à peu de l'obscurité
qui est la fin des choses.

Puis
l'argent
vient dans l'herbe
et les aiguilles des pins
assoiffées de feu ;
        le feu prend enfin
à la mer et arrache au sable sa couleur ;
— entre les buissons
de feu,
les planches disjointes :
les mouvements inlassables de l'eau —
devant tes plaies, Sébastien,

to join,
the blank eyes
that the dancing light
has left.

(Saint Sebastian
pierced by too many wounds)
Kneeling
on the fine, bright grass,
when this earth disappears,
a large stain on the eyes,
on the tongue
—the varied taste
of black fruits is lost;
the thorns,
the leaves
and the steps
buried
little by little by the darkness
that is the end of things.

Then
silver
comes into the grass
and the pine needles
thirsty for fire;
          the fire sweeps
to the sea and strips the sand of its color;
—between the bushes
fire,
disjointed planks:
the tireless motion of the water—
before your wounds, Sebastian,

le visage levé ;
le châtaignier,
son encens pris à la nuit,
le rivage opposé,
net,
et, dans la contemplation,
ce martyre.

Comment se tenir
devant les nuages sur le mur,
la mer de métal et d'encre
qui vient avec le froid,
traversée des feux épars
et la route battue, sous les réverbères oranges ?

lifted face;
the chestnut tree,
its incense gathered into the night,
the far bank,
clear,
and in contemplation,
this martyr.

How to hold it together
before the clouds on the wall,
the sea of metal and ink
that comes with the cold,
covered by scattered fires
and the battered path, beneath the orange street lamps?

Trans. J.B. Anderson

AU MOMENT DE MOURIR

Ton corps s'élance en arrière,
tombe,
se perd ;
et tu vois la ville se renverser,
dans le tournoiement
de ta chute.
Avant de perdre connaissance,
tu avais
père et frère,
avant l'encerclement
des serpents de fer ;
quelquefois tes yeux, de profil,
si petits, avaient ce gonflement
— il serait là —
avaient un reflet de lac
lointain,
dans un visage
allongé du Greco.
La froideur prend et tord.
Des mains de feu bleu glacé tombent derrière
la ville et les montagnes,
cette pâleur
tendue
et traversée d'ombres
— ces nuages se déchirent —
tandis que le cheval rentre vers la porte
de la ville
et que le serpent
enroulé mord le corps

AT THE MOMENT OF DYING

Your body thrusts backward,
falls,
loses its way
and you see the city overturned
in the whirling
of your fall.
Before losing consciousness,
you had
father and brother,
before the encircling
of steel serpents;
sometimes your eyes, in profile,
so small, had that swelling
—he was there—
had a lake's reflection
distant,
in an elongated
face by Greco.
Cold seizes and twists.
Hands of icy blue fire fall behind
the city and the mountains,
this pallor
stretched
and shot through by shadows
—these clouds tear themselves—
while the horse returns toward the gate
of the city
and the serpent
coiled bites the body

nu et blanc,
traversé de mort
dans la torsion verticale, puis te déséquilibre.

*

Je passai les ombres
jusqu'à l'arrondi du bar :
des éclats de cuivre,
au loin,
éclairèrent les zones imaginaires
qui brûlèrent soudain au feu
froid de verre.

L'éclat des sons
dura longtemps :
j'entendais
la texture du bruit amplifié,
et le chant de
la nuit mêlée à ce jour,
inverse de la nuit
et non vrai jour.

Mon regard acide connut
la lumière qui n'altère pas, mais
donne pâleur, éclat
au teint où court
la roseur de la joie ou
le bleu de la mort.

*

nude and white,
shot through by death
in vertical torsion, then unbalances you.

*

I passed shadows
up to the curve of the bar:
glints of copper,
in the distance,
lit up imaginary zones
that burned suddenly in the burning
cold of glass.

The burst of sounds
lasted a long time;
I heard
the texture of the noise amplified,
and the song of
night mixed with this day,
opposite of night
and not true day.

My sour glance knew
the light that does not alter, but
lends paleness, gleam
tinged where there runs
the rosiness of joy or
the blue of death.

*

Les mains saintes se touchent presque,
le bord d'une aile
ou les cassures du tissu —
formant comme un rocher ou une grotte —
enveloppent les dormeurs étendus.
Des nuages se déchirent en passant
devant la clarté
de l'Esprit.
Il y a aussi
les paliers et les collines aux contours neigeux
sous la lune et
les cyprès argent.
Le serpent est là.

Déjà la perte, et la beauté
croît ;
dans la voix, les yeux,
il y a déjà autre chose :
l'inconnu dans le connu,
ce lien
serrant les membres tendus
dans sa force de mort
et
le serpent qui s'approche,
la morsure.
Le sillon creuse le corps et,
devant la ville haute,
tu perds l'équilibre comme tu avais perdu le droit regard,
levé,
égaré, au ciel flou,
plein des formes mauvaises
des nuages,
les bras raidis

The sacred hands almost touch
the edge of a wing
or the shreds of fabric
forming like a boulder or a grotto—
they envelop the stretched-out sleepers.
Clouds tear themselves apart in passing
before the clarity
of the Spirit.
There are also
levels and hills with snowy contours
beneath the moon and
silver cypresses.
The snake is there.

Already loss, and the beauty
grows;
in the voice, in the eyes,
there is already something else:
the unknown in the known,
this link
locking the stretched limbs
in the force of death
and
the snake that approaches,
the bite.
The furrow hollows the body and,
before the lofty city
you lose your balance as you lost clear sight,
lifted,
lost, to the blurred sky,
filled with evil shapes
of clouds,
arms stiffened

ne pouvant te dégager de la capture.
Les constructions sont comme un règne rêvé,
les arbres floconneux et le cheval rond
comme un rêve de douceur.
Je ne vois plus le chemin vers la porte de la ville.
Toi, mourant,
te détournes.

not able to released you from capture.
Constructions are like a dreamed kingdom,
the wispy trees and the round horse
like a dream of gentleness.
I no longer see the path toward the door of the city.
You, dying,
turn away.

Trans. M. Kallet

UN FRUIT ÉTRANGE

Un pylône aux tiges en croix
figure un gibet, fanal rouge, dressé on ne sait où,
qui tremble et siffle au vent de l'autoroute ;
tranchée, puis coulée, de loin, sur les collines et les fleuves, qui
    va
dans les villes électriques
sans remparts.
La musique, à la radio, tremble aussi, se brouille et se perd
    dans la nuit
grésillante
qu'elle ornait : rosée noire sur le filet assassin.

Treillage,
lierre aux feuilles
forgées
sur la lumière d'une veille sans fin, fading.
L'asphalte brille,
les jointures des os se dissolvent ;
au ciel on voit
les marches dégradées, grises des rafales ;
mais la flamme brûle encore,
c'est la fleur écarlate
— en elle se mue la mort —
qu'incendia
l'étincelle écartée
du mouvement stellaire.

Oui, ce pays est beau, dit le condamné,
ce jour aussi, dans les herbes hautes
de la prairie ; je me souviens maintenant
des iris nocturnes, du souffle de l'attente ;
car nous fûmes touchés

A STRANGE FRUIT

A pylon with crossed shafts
looks like the gallows, a red lantern, erected who knows
   where,
trembling and hissing in the highway's wind;
clearly delineated, and then melting away, from afar, on the
   hills and the rivers passing through
the electric cities
without walls.
The music, on the radio, also wavers, scrambles and then gets
   lost in the crackling night
that it adorned: black dew on the killing rope.

Trellis,
ivy with leaves
forged
in the light of an endless vigil, fade-out.
The asphalt glitters,
the bones' joints dissolve;
in the sky we see
worn steps, gray from the gusts;
but the flame burns again,
it is the scarlet flower
—in which death changes—
that burned
the wayward spark
of stellar movement.

Yes, this country is beautiful, says the condemned man,
this day too, in the high grass
of the prairie; I remember now
nocturnal irises, breath of expectation;
for we were touched

de Qui écartèle les nuages
et partage les fleuves.

La clé perdue tinte encore
sur les pavés de la place à la fontaine
— Séville —
les rires hurlants ouvrent
des rues blanches dans la ville.
Et lorsque, dans l'après-midi,
on avance, comme dans les hautes herbes,
et qu'on s'agenouille
là, devant,
on ne peut rappeler
le rire ni la danse
de leur oubli ;
tout rompt
à cette tentative,
et du heurt des êtres
naît on ne sait
quelle bête.

Le soleil a brûlé,
ce jour-là, comme la salamandre.
Le lendemain, devant la plaie de ce corps
creusé et noirci, nous avons entendu
les cris sauvages de la vie.

Ils sont
autour de la maison,
les maîtres des liens
serrant jusqu'à étrangler
les gorges.

by the One who parts the clouds
and divides the rivers.

The lost key still rings
on the cobblestones of the plaza with the fountain
—Seville—
the hysterical laughs open
the city's white streets.
And one afternoon,
when we go forward, as through grass,
and we kneel
there, in front,
we can remember
neither the laugh nor the dance
of their forgetfulness;
everything falls apart
at this attempt,
and from the collision of beings
is born some unknown
beast.

The sun burned,
that day, like the salamander.
The next day, before the wound of this hollowed and
    blackened
corpse, we heard
the wild cries of life.

They are
around the house,
the rope masters
close, strangle
the throats.

Trans. J.B. Anderson

IDA, EN MIROIR

À *Paul Bley*,
pianiste de jazz

Les lances hautes des cannes
ombrées de gris, sous le vent
s'agitent, l'épi luisant.
Certaines ont cassé sur le ruisseau franchi,
elles bruissent.

Dans le brouhaha de la salle
du restaurant,
le sourire, par jeu,
change ton visage.
Des feuilles-sabres se croisent,
disent
la distance jouée,
l'inquiétude
du baiser peint
qui déchire et renoue.

Vois, la montagne, en pleine lumière, s'efface,
vaporisée, mais la mer se couvre d'un nuage
formant un sommet brumeux.
Plus loin que le golfe,
ces chaînes s'étagent
avec la douceur d'un reflet :
la fleur-flocon refleurit
dans le panorama inversé.
L'étendue gris-argent de la mer
se trouble,
elle porte maintenant des yeux peints, les taches

IDA, IN THE MIRROR

To Paul Bley,
jazz pianist

The tall cane spears
shadowed in grey rustled by the wind
shake, shining sword.
Some break on the forded stream,
They whisper.

In the clamor of
a restaurant
a smile, playfully,
changes your face.
Sword-leaves clash,
tell
the played distance,
the worry
of the painted kiss
that pulls asunder and ties together.

See, the mountain, in full light, fades,
evaporated, but the sea covers itself with a cloud
forming a misty summit.
Beyond the gulf,
these mountain ranges pile up
with the gentleness of a reflection:
the flake-flower flowers again
in the inverted landscape.
The silver-grey expanse of the sea
grows restless,
it now wears painted eyes, the dull stains

ternes de nuages,
et se ride de l'agitation acide
d'un regret pris dans son flux.

Ce paysage aux habitations
uniformes, que traverse le train
de banlieue,
est devenu le symbole
de l'accord profond et momentané
avec la terre poussiéreuse
où,
toi jouant,
l'appréhension
qui naît à regarder trembler
le contour des choses
par instants se lève.

of the clouds,
and ripples in the acid agitation
of a regret seized in flux.

This landscape of uniform
apartment blocks that the commuter rail
crosses
has become the symbol
of a deep and momentary accord
with the dusty earth
where,
when you play,
the anguish
born to bear witness to the trembling
edges of things
once in a while disappears.

Trans. J.B. Anderson

TOMBEAU DU PRINTEMPS

Le visage se détournant
de la pensée
peut encore
s'enfoncer dans la peine,
ce noir
ouvre une spirale
et voici, tête première,
la chute
— tandis qu'au cœur,
cette blancheur,
la lame, brille
d'une douleur nouvelle —
vers la non-conscience,
pas même la toupie de la mort ;

nos pas vont
dans les mêmes rues :
ce n'est plus la nuit,
au feuillage forgé et tremblant,
porté sur le mur par les phares des bateaux-mouches,
voici un arbre traversé de soleil,
tout est changé,
il faut, défaillant,
entrer sous les arcades de pierre
où l'orgue écrase
le devenir
de ce qui fut :
tombeau du printemps
en été,
abandon

SPRING'S GRAVE

The face turning away
from thought
can still
sink into pain,
this blackness
opens up a vortex,
and look, head first,
the fall
—while in the heart,
this whiteness,
the knife edge, blazes
with a new pain—
towards unconsciousness,
not even the spinning top of death;

our steps
in the same streets:
it is no longer the night
of trembling and wrought foliage
thrown onto the wall by the floodlights of the *bateaux-
    mouches,*
here is a tree filled with sunlight,
everything is changed,
we must, stumbling,
enter beneath the arcades of stone
where the organ crushes
the coming into being
of what once was:
spring's grave
in summer,
abandoned

à cet écrasement, renoncement ;
alors, vers les arcatures,
le regard se perd,
et la pierre s'affinant,
touchée par le rayon électrique,
figure

une végétation neuve
— une allée, un mouvement
sous les tiges
entrelacées —
qui tremble
inaperçue
jusque-là ;

et la foule des gens dehors, les chanteurs
avec les sons des
Fender Rhodes ;

on peut s'arrêter, entre les motos,
appuyés au mur
et c'est à nouveau vivre d'ainsi voir,
et plus que vivre d'entendre autour
les hurlements et les rires
des promeneurs anachroniques ;

c'est la fleur de fuchsia
qu'on ne peut toucher
et qui bouge
sous le souffle
de l'Au-delà :
on y entre déjà,
au son du vent

to this crushing renunciation;
and so the gaze loses itself
in decorative arcades,
and stone becomes more delicate,
caressed by electric light,
figuring

a new vegetation
—an alley, a movement
beneath interwoven
stems—
that trembles
imperceptible
till then;

and the crowd of people outside, the singers
with the sounds of
Fender Rhodes;

we can stop, between some motorcycles,
resting against a wall
and to see like this is like living again,
and more than living to listen
to the shouts and laughs
of the strollers out of time;

it is the fuchsia flower
that we cannot touch
and that moves
in the breeze
from the Beyond:
we are already inside,
in the sound of the wind

dans les herbes et les feuilles,
qui ne soulève pas
l'ombre étendue
de plus en plus vaste ;
pensée
à laquelle tout se lie,
la fleur est là,
elle préfigure l'artifice
flamboyant sur la nuit
qu'on attend au bord du fleuve invisible.

in the grass and the leaves,
that do not lift
the shadow that
grows and grows;
thought
to which everything clings,
the flower is there,
it prefigures the artifice
flaming against the night
that we wait for on the bank of the invisible river.

Trans. J.B. Anderson

LA VILLE DÉSENCHANTÉE

Avions transnocturnes, glissement
des voitures, paroles, verre brisé,
cris lointains et sifflets...
brume des rires, portes
qu'on claque...
la nuit se fait-elle silencieuse et obscure
dans la fièvre et la discorde, et les sons s'intensifiant ?
En face, la paroi, cernée de ciel,
s'assombrit encore, sonneries
de téléphone, klaxons, boîte à ordures et fenêtres heurtées,
la porte tremble et, plus loin que les cris, la rumeur, grossie
   d'appels, bat,
derrière les conversations plus proches,
la télé : ses ombres bleues gigantesques
tressautent sur les murs qu'elles recouvrent...
la ville se construit,
par l'étagement des sons,
citadelle idéale, remuant de bêtes enchaînées
et du flux des esprits qui s'éveillent dans la chaleur et l'alcool.

Je te vis ainsi et
je baissai les yeux.

Plus tard,
nous sortirions de la maison
où tout s'était dit, parmi les fleurs frêles
chues — la neige rose de ce jour-là —
et les rues défigurées s'ouvriraient
à notre errance.

THE DISENCHANTED CITY

          Red-eye flights, skidding
cars, words, broken glass,
distant screams and catcalls…
a fog of laughter, slamming
doors…
is the night becoming silent and dark
in fever and discord and intensifying sounds?
In front, the wall, enclosed in sky,
is still dark, the noise from
telephones, car horns, ashcans and shattered windows,
the door rattles and, beyond the screams, whispers filled with
    pleading, bangs,
behind the nearest conversations,
the TV: its gigantic blue shadows
twitching all over the walls…
The city builds itself
through the layering of sounds,
ideal citadel, bristling with chained animals
and the flux of spirits that wakes up in heat and alcohol.

          I saw you like this and
I lowered my eyes.

          Later,
we would leave the house
where everything had been said, among the frail broken
flowers—that day's pink snow—
and the disfigured streets would open
to our wandering.

Ma joie était tombée au bord du quai
du métro, à attendre. Tous parlaient
une langue incompréhensible.
Les rues tournaient brusquement,
décorées d'arbres absurdes
et ma colère montait, par vagues.
Il fallut s'en retourner, nous ne vîmes pas le parc.

Je te savais maintenant
Heureux toujours uni désaccordé.

Des barges
semblaient immobilisées au milieu du fleuve,
les rives offraient leur désolation
à nos pensées de chute
de l'ancien monde et d'avènement du désespoir,
mais nous riions encore
de passer dans un désordre de ruines rénovées
et d'épaves modernes.

My joy had fallen at the tube's
edge, left waiting. Everyone spoke
an incomprehensible language.
The streets violently lurched,
decorated with absurd trees
and my anger grew, in waves.
We had to turn around, we did not see the park.

       I know you now
Heureux toujours uni désaccordé.

Barges
seem immobilized in the middle of the river,
the riverside offered its desolation
to our thoughts of the old world's
fall and despair's triumph,
but we will laugh again
as we passed amidst the disorder of renovated ruins
and modern wreckage.

Trans. J.B. Anderson

II

II

NOS JEUX TRAVERSÉS

Tressaillements,
ni les buissons, ni rien, au dehors,
n'est en feu ; un badigeon,
ravage accompli d'incendie,
couvre tout de sa nuit superficielle,
durée obscure où le réveil clignote ;

      au loin, les collines solitaires,
traversées d'autoroutes magnifiques
par où rejoindre d'autres villes, l'océan ;
le fracas du train, soudain,
le damier vibre avec l'espace, ruinant
nos arrangements savants.

Le matin aura le bercement souriant et artificiel
des palmes contre un mur blanc,
tu relèveras doucement
les figurines de nos jeux traversés.

OUR INTERRUPTED GAMES

Startled,
neither the brush nor anything else out there
is burning; whitewash,
the fire's successful destruction,
blankets everything in its superficial night,
a dark time when the alarm clock flickers;

      in the distance the solitary hills,
crisscrossed by magnificent highways
that reach other cities, the ocean;
suddenly the train's roar,
the checkerboard vibrates with space, ruining
our knowing arrangements.

Morning will have the pleasant and fake swaying
of palm leaves against a white wall,
you will gently pick up
the pieces of interrupted games.

Trans. J.B. Anderson

LA CHASSE

Image tremblée, danse,
son feu incite
et prend, entraîne
au bord du lac, plus loin
que les barrières, dans l'herbe haute et luisante.
Comme ton visage change !
grave, quasi immobile ;
l'ombre de l'arbre a bougé,
le froid de la nuit ;
scènes et signes sur
ton corps voué au regard,
qui traverse le temps et le change,
sans repos, pas de lieu où
s'asseoir, des hôtels, des guichets,
ni où boire, les arbres déployés et dissolvant l'interdit de
    plomb ;
on ne peut plus avancer, tourner seulement
en rond, toutes les routes barrées par
la nuit,
les animaux s'ébrouent, s'approchent,
la voiture
...

THE HUNT

The trembling image dances,
its fire incites
and takes, drags
to the edge of the lake, beyond
the fence, in the shining high grass.
How your face changes!
grave, almost immobile;
the tree's shadow moved,
the evening cold;
scenes and signs on
your body given over to a gaze,
that crosses time and changes it,
restless, no place
to sit, hotels, counters,
nothing to drink, the unfurled trees dissolving the leaden
    prohibition;
we can't go forward anymore, only turn
in circles, all roads blocked by
the night,
animals are snorting, and getting closer,
the car
...

Trans. J.B. Anderson

III

III

ME SOUVENANT DU BAPTÊME DE PIERO

Le soir s'obscurcit, les cloches anciennes sombrent
derrière les faces noires et illuminées des immeubles,
au bord d'un fleuve bétonné, résurgent,
d'une voie ferrée à l'abandon gagnée enfin par l'herbe ;
l'espace entre les poutres grises
laisse voir du sable, des flaques :
les dernières couleurs vivent dans cet interstice opalin.
Les nuages s'écartent,
la lune et l'étoile tendent un ciel derrière
les lettres OXO
et les fumées ininterrompues de l'incinérateur à ordures ;
le bruit est surtout celui du vent,
sur ces voies en construction, boueuses,
où les madriers s'alignent dans
l'eau de pluie,
il va en vagues vers la perspective
grillagée des moulins et des frigorifiques médiévaux,
   grandioses,
criards, tagués.
Sous le ciel déchiré et beau,
clignotant d'avions, porteur d'astres et vaste,
marcher au bord de la ville à vif,
ce chantier, c'est retraverser ce jardin artificiel
où le carillon de l'église nous rappela
que tout avait basculé
et, qu'inséparable de l'impression d'exister,
il y a cet élargissement de souffrance et de merveilleux :
la cascade brumeuse à la vertu inconnue,
son scintillement ; nous nous tenons au bord,

REMEMBERING PIERO'S BAPTISM

Night is falling, old bells fade away
behind the black lit-up faces of apartment buildings
next to a stream filled with concrete engulfing
an abandoned railroad track that is overtaken in the end by
    grass;
in between the grey railroad ties
you can see sand, puddles:
the last colors survive in this opalescent interstice.
Clouds part,
the moon and a star pin the sky behind
the letters OXO
and the garbage incinerator's endless smoke;
the noise is mostly wind
on these muddy, partially built tracks,
where beams line up in
the rainwater,
it surges towards the gridded
horizon of garish medieval mills and refrigerators
covered in graffiti.
Beneath the torn-up and beautiful sky,
winking with planes, bearer of planets and stars, vast,
to walk beside this construction site,
the city open and raw, is to recross the artificial garden
where the church bells reminded us
that everything has been overturned
and that, inseparable from the sense of existence,
there is this expansion of suffering and of the marvelous:
the misty waterfall its essence unknown
glittering; we stand at the edge

pour le baptême,
dans le dénuement du cri.
Nouveauté sauvage, océanique : notre perte et le vent qui nous
transperce.

to be baptized
in an impoverishing cry.
Savage novelty, oceanic: our loss, and the wind that pierces us.

Trans. J.B. Anderson

NOS OISEAUX

Le dessin prend vie,
une branche de givre
se détache de la vitre
et penche vers les herbes
ses fleurs lourdes ;
la nuit même cède
à l'aube fausse d'une lune mauve,
maladive ;
la prairie a
la douceur du
velours, entre les
arbres noirs, où la neige tient
encore, des oiseaux
très bien peints
commencent leurs cris
proches, puis lointains,
chantent le jour feint
de ce renversement ;

la pelouse est jonchée
d'ardoises
et, sur fond de pluie
continue, le jardin
porte le tronc brisé
du poirier ;
qu'aurait pu être l'aube ?
un froissement
de l'étoffe de la prairie,
le déplacement
du voile doux
avivant

OUR BIRDS

The design comes to life,
a branch of frost
detaches itself from the pane
and lavishes its heavy flowers
on the grass;
even the night yields
to the false dawn of a moon, mauve
and diseased;
the grassland is
as gentle as
velvet, between the
black trees, where snow still
clings, finely painted
birds
begin to chirp
near, then far,
singing the sham day
of this reversal;

the lawn is carpeted
with pieces of slate
and, against a background of
constant rain, the garden
contains the broken trunk
of a pear tree;
what must daybreak have been like?
a rustling
of the meadow's fabric,
the shifting
of a gentle veil,
quickening

le contour des maisons,
ou l'envol
d'oiseaux vivants ?

Le Destin est peint,
sur l'écu
du chevalier tombé :
voici les fleurs de l'Oubli,
du sommeil
et de l'engourdissement,
le velours moiré irrite
la paume fatiguée ;
Noir,
Blanc :
damier de lettres
échangées
dans un roman,
où l'on croit
au matin,
n'ayant
que la froideur
nocturne
et nul apaisement ;

l'image
héraldique
porte
le tronc brisé
sur fond
de sable,
où le sang
rouge
est bu,

the contour of the houses,
or the flight
of living birds?

Destiny is painted,
on the shield
of the fallen knight:
here are the flowers of Forgetfulness,
of sleep
and of numbness,
the glassy velvet irritates
the tired palm;
Black,
White:
checkerboard of letters
exchanged
in a novel,
where we believe
in morning,
having nothing
but the night's
cold
and no relief;

the heraldic
image
features
the broken trunk
on a background
of sable,
where red
blood
is drunk,

où la tempête,
muette et violente,
avec son souffle de bête,
a défait
le drapé lunaire,
dévoilant ainsi les
mots : Peine,
Liesse,
et fasciné nos mains
vivantes.

where the tempest,
mute and violent,
with its animal panting,
undid
the moon's beautifully hung garment,
thereby unveiling the
words: Punishment,
Jubilation,
and charmed our living
hands.

Trans. J.B. Anderson

TRANSLATION

D'un rêve, la texture blanche,
rideau soulevé par le souffle du dehors ;
longtemps après les détours de l'esprit
pris dans l'écheveau, l'indécidable
bourrasque des voitures, camions,
remorques qui tressautent ;
la maison tremble à leur passage,
les images, les images du passé recomposé
cèdent,
c'est le jour enfin,
tu entres parmi les branches
entrecroisées, les oiseaux
alternent leurs appels,
leurs chants se mêlent et se répondent
et la conscience naît de la déploration,
d'une voie allant
du passé clair,
tien,
mien,
par la séparation,
à la présence sans faille,
toi m'accompagnant,
moi n'hésitant pas sur le chemin ; maintenant
le matin est sur les champs, aux fenêtres blanches ;
sur l'horizon,
rameaux noirs entrelacés,

feuilles et oiseaux chantant,
la maison, les voitures,
sur la route de Chartres.

TRANSLATION

From a dream, the white texture,
curtain raised by the breath of beyond;
long after the detours of the mind
caught in the tangle, the indeterminate
jumble of cars, trucks,
tows which jolt;
the house trembles at their passage,
the images, the images of the past recomposed
yield,
it's finally day,
you enter amid branches
interlaced, the birds
alternate their calls,
their songs mingle and answer
and consciousness is born from the lament,
from a route going
from the clear past,
yours,
mine,
by separation,
to presence without fault,
you accompanying me,
me not hesitating on the path; now
morning is on the fields, at the white windows;
on the horizon
black twigs interlaced,

leaves and birdsong,
the house, the cars,
on the road to Chartres.

Trans. M. Kallet

CARTE POSTALE

À Eric Dolphy

Stries, couleurs cloisonnées d'or strident,
rayons mystiques,
des nuages bleu-gris pleuvent,
se délitent, sur les bandes roses, étirées,
craie grasse de la mer réverbérante,
sauvage mauve et violet profond,
fusion nouvelle des teintes tendres puis
plus sombres figées par la chute du soleil
disparu là derrière,
au bord du rivage habité où la mer
passe la digue, pulvérise les cubes gris des maisons,
dernières avancées solides
sous la grande roue broyeuse et enflammée
des chatoiements de la Fire Waltz

Fire Waltz est aussi un bar :
les voitures se garent, tonnerre des galets,
le large — là-bas, c'est l'Amérique ! —
après la porte de métal gaufré,
l'ondoiement le long du bar entre les tables,
le reggae à fond jusqu'au billard immense,
les hauts tableaux modernes,
les baies vitrées, le coucher de soleil,
l'impression du dehors,
s'estompent dans la tiédeur,
le grésillement des baffles.

POSTCARD

To Eric Dolphy

Streaks, colors split into blaring gold,
mystic rays,
pouring from blue-grey clouds,
decompose in rose strips, stretched
thick chalk of reverberating sea,
wild mauve and deep purple,
new fusion of tender shades then
more somber congealed by sun's fall
disappearing back there,
at the edge of the inhabited shore where the sea
passes the dam, pulverizes the grey cubes of houses,
last solid bulwarks
under the great inflamed and pounding wheel
of the shifting hues of Fire Waltz.

Fire Waltz is also a bar:
cars park, pounding of cobblestones
the open sea—over there! America—
inside the door of honeycombed metal,
shadowing the bar's length between tables
reggae revved up to the huge billiard table,
tall modern paintings,
bay windows, sunset,
the impression of outdoors,
blur in the lukewarm air,
speaker cones crackling.

Trans. M. Kallet

RIVAGE FRAGMENTÉ

Comment reconnaître ce rivage froid de cendres
où le sable secoue ses éclats,
disparu maintenant sous la lave,
les vagues contraires qui recouvrent leurs transparences
présagent un orage,
ou lorsque, l'eau retirée, des plaques
en fusion se creusent
de ruisseaux arborescents allant au flot,
en cet instant, sans bruit,
seul, un moteur au loin,
ce recul incompréhensible en golfe,
des couleurs de coquille reflétées sur l'eau,
les nuages gonflés, les chiens
là-bas et le dos rosé de quelques caravanes
entre les arbres, les maisons muettes ;
le sable durci en ondulations gris de tôle, inondées par
    places,
et imprimées de traces de pattes et de pas :
les véliplanchistes, en effet,
dans leurs combinaisons se débattent
avec leur aile
de plastique,
les familles jouent au sable, au ballon, à l'eau,
l'homme au chien court,
d'autres sont allongés,
aussi calmes qu'au bord d'un lac.
Sous les feux alternés des phares dans la nuit qui fut
nappe réverbérante, les villas s'allument,
un bidon, une sandale, pris dans les algues,
marquent un relief,
relief aussi ces amas de débris nacrés, rejetés

A BROKEN SHORELINE

How to recognize this cold shoreline of ashes
where the sand flaunts its radiance,
now vanished beneath the lava,
criss-crossing waves cloud the depths
forecasting a storm,
or when, the water pulled back, joined
plates are hollowed out
with tree-like streams draining into the sea,
right now, without a sound,
alone, a motor in the distance,
this senseless return to the gulf
of seashell colors reflected in the water,
swollen clouds, dogs
over there and the salmon colored backs of some RVs
between the trees, mute houses;
the sand hardened into sheet-metal grey waves, flooded in
    places,
and dimpled with paw prints and foot prints:
the windsurfers
in their formations are basically fighting
with their plastic
wing,
families are playing in the sand, balls, water,
the man with his dog is jogging,
others are stretched out,
as calm as if they were beside a lake.
Below the lighthouses' signals pulsing through a night that was
a blinding sheet, the villas light up,
a can, a sandal, tangled in the seaweed,
indicate a rise in the land,
as is this mass of nacreous debris thrown up

par saccades, sous les lampes,
les voitures, portières ouvertes, à la radio :
Well we do shine on
Like the moon and the stars and the sun,
rangées, surplombent l'eau contenue, dans une
étendue à la montée régulière.

fitfully, under the lamps,
the cars, open doors, on the radio:
Well we do shine on
Like the moon and the stars and the sun
that plumb the trapped water, spaced
evenly at regular depths.

Trans. J.B. Anderson

IV

IV

ÉCLAT MÉTALLIQUE

L'eau combattait la lumière ;
cependant ils jouaient
et les coquillages brisés ne blessaient pas leurs pieds ;
le mur tombait,
mur d'eau sur cette ville blanche, fortifiée
de récifs et d'immeubles,
sur la puanteur des algues
mêlées aux planches arrachées, pneus,
bouchons à vis, gants de caoutchouc décolorés,
débris de plastique, amas de cordages ou de filets,
sur la lanière, l'éponge, la fougère brune incrustée au sol,
les insectes et les oiseaux.

Chaque aube sera plus fraîche,
se lèvera, ornée de celles qui l'ont précédée, portera
le ciel, compliqué des nuages changeants, dans l'eau qui les
    reflète
— tout reflet nouveau teint l'eau qui prend la lumière ;
sur l'eau des lacs, qui repose dans les cônes volcaniques,
se peint un ciel immobile.

Tout s'obscurcit.
Cette clarté acide, au goût d'eau d'oranger
porte en elle la corruption des sources,
de l'eau glaciaire
qui rougit les membres douloureux,
où trop de fleurs blanches, pelucheuses ont puisé leur forme
    d'étoile,
— cueillies trop haut dans l'aura des cimes —

METALLIC FLASH

Water battled light;
yet they played
and the broken shells didn't wound their feet;
the wall fell,
wall of water on this bleached city, fortified
with reefs and flats
on the stink of algae
mixed with torn boards, tires,
corkscrews, gloves of discolored rubber,
plastic debris, heaps of rope or of thread
on the strip, the sponge, the brown fern
        encrusted in the ground,
insects and birds.

Each dawn will be fresher,
will break, adorned with those that preceded, will carry
the sky, complicated by changing clouds in the water that
    reflects them
—all new reflection tints the water that catches light;
on the lake water that remains in volcanic cones,
a still sky paints itself.

Everything darkens.
This acid clarity, with the flavor of orange trees
carries in itself the corruption of the springs,
the glacial water
which reddens sorrowful limbs,
where too many white flowers, ragged have spent their star
    shape,
—picked too high in the aura of the summits—

et la souffrance à boire cette eau
résonne déjà en nous et nous brise
si elle n'est renouvelée et accrue.

Étoiles dans les ruisseaux.
Le vent veut des coups de feu
pour disperser les avions brillants
derrière les branches nouées de bourgeons,
dans le silence où se séparent la pensée et le corps,
et dissiper leur traîne.

Écroulement des murs ; fenêtres nouvelles ;
au loin, les fumées dans le jour jeune,
quelques maisons grises.
Mais ce jour n'a rien d'une aube : les murs explosent.
Les hauts murs déferlent vers nous
— lutte pour être encore,
malgré le trait vertical qui frappe de lueurs orageuses ;
au-dessus de nous, tout autour, trop de clarté.

and the suffering from drinking this water
resonates in us now and breaks us
unless it is renewed and restored.

Stars in the streams.
The wind wants gunfire
to disperse its bright planes
behind branches whose knots are buds,
in the silence which separates thought and body,
and to dissipate their train.

Crumbling of walls; new windows;
in the distance, plumes of smoke in the new day,
some grey houses.
But this day has nothing of dawn: walls explode.
The high walls unfurl toward us
—struggle to still exist,
despite the vertical stroke which strikes with stormy glints;
above us, all around, too much clarity.

Trans. M. Kallet

SEPTEMBRE

Silhouettes fugitives, au cœur d'espaces barrés
de signes, saturés de chemins,
rayés déjà, d'empreintes, de traces
de passages.

Or, la pensée de l'inconnu serre
la gorge à l'entrée de cette allée des hauts rêves, réverbérante
  et ratissée...

ce sont seulement les alentours, mais déjà nous imaginons un
  séjour autre,
un séjour agréable, car nous en gardons le souvenir ;

avancer doucement, maintenant,
dans une pensée multiple, ainsi,
en temps de guerre et d'amour, avec, en esprit, la beauté,
ce fil cassé à regret, toujours repris
par l'interrogation, la demande douce.

Reliés à peine au dehors, nous pouvons tenter encore de
  parcourir la distance
qui en éloigne et peser cette ombre profonde, enfantine et
  inquiète
qui s'avance, unique et gracieuse
dans la clarté blanche du soleil d'hiver, plaqué sur les toits,
  dessinant
à contre-jour les cheminées d'un autre temps,
ceinturées de métal pour supporter les disques
blancs des antennes paraboliques
et qui délivrent ce sens de l'ancien — seul lieu
où j'imagine que nous puissions vivre.

SEPTEMBER

Fugitive silhouettes in the midst of spaces
crammed with signs, filled with paths,
already lined with footprints, with marks
of passage.

Yet, the thought of the unknown seizes
the throat at the entrance of this avenue of lofty dreams,
    bright and raked over...

these are only the surroundings, but we already imagine
    another journey,
a pleasant journey, because we remember some;

go forth gently, now,
in a multifarious thought, thus,
in times of war and love, with, in the spirit, beauty,
this thread broken with regret, always taken up again
through inquiry, a gentle question.

Barely reconnected outside, we can still attempt to close the
    distance
that separates us from it and ponder childish and ill at ease
    this deep shadow
that gets closer, solitary and graceful
in the winter sun's white clarity gilding the roofs, sketching
the chimneys of another time against the light,
belted with metal to support the
satellite antennae's white disks
and which deliver this sense of the ancient—only place
where I imagine we could live.

Les grues plantées parmi les immeubles
tournent dans la rumeur
de midi, des klaxons, des déménagements,
des voix, des cris d'enfants,
des réponses vives seules entendues
ici, loin de la vie, de ce combat.
Lisant, dans ce flot,
le mouvement tournant de cette grue,
les traces de pluie
et les constellations poussiéreuses
d'anciens ciels,
que la grande clarté fait paraître sur les vitres,
de loin en loin vient la certitude
de reprendre ce qui a été commencé,
de recommencer à parler
avec et sans mots, d'évoquer
un lieu inconnu encore où ces
signes peuvent nous mener,
réconciliés, peut-être,
avec ce perpétuel chantier,
ce remuement profond sans lequel
ne va pas la vie,
ces échos stridents
et qui sont la texture des jours ;
en cet instant, de loin,
la rue est tranchée de violence
et de bruit, j'ai hâte d'y être aussi ;

trame continue mais lâche, croisée de brins immatériels :
ces pas à déchiffrer et suivre ;
puis l'impossibilité se noue dans la hâte,
il faut s'en aller : il n'y a plus d'émotion dans les voix
    lointaines.

The cranes planted among the buildings
turn amidst the
midday sounds, car horns, displacements,
voices, crying children,
heated exchanges heard only
here, far from life, from this battle.
Reading, in this flood,
the turning movement of this crane,
the traces of rain
and the dusty constellations
of former skies
that the sharp light conjures on the panes,
from far away comes the certitude
of returning to what was begun,
of resuming speech
with and without words, of evoking
a place still unknown where these
signs might lead us,
reconciled perhaps
with this perpetual construction site,
this profound movement without which
life does not go on,
these strident echoes
which are the stuff of days;
in this instant, from afar,
the road is gashed with violence
and sound, I long to be there too;

continuous but slack thread, crossed with immaterial strands:
these footsteps to be deciphered and followed;
and then the impossibility is knotted in haste,
we must get out of here: there is no more emotion in these far
   away voices.

L'histoire est à retraverser :
chemin lourd de ce qui est et de ce qui sera, avancée
en lisière où chaque pas est décisif dans la haute
demeure blanche qui ne nous appartient plus.

La nuit tombe en cascade
et les cœurs ouverts reçoivent sa fraîcheur,
tandis que demeurent sur les façades
noires des immeubles d'en face
des fenêtres allumées
où la veille est espoir, impossible abandon
au repos, refus et tentative de l'emporter sur le temps ;
nous aurons soif toute cette nuit,
tournant nos corps enfiévrés
jusqu'au matin, tandis que le cœur
battant à la nouvelle entendue
ne pourra s'apaiser :
oiseau palpitant de son propre chant,
encagé et avide du matin
où fleurit la fleur rouge somptueuse
et éphémère, continuation de la pensée,
accrochée à l'appui forgé et noir
de la fenêtre,
fleur du seuil de la vision qui saisit
avant d'entrer dans la vie renouvelée
des premières heures du jour ;
constance est le nom de cette fleur nourrie
de pluie et de gaz, accrochée
au bord, au moment du passage,
lèvres qui parlent
de durée, malgré
l'éclosion fragile et la flétrissure certaine.

History is to be relived:
heavy path of what is and what shall be, thrust
into the edge of the forest where every step is decisive in the
   high
white building that no longer belongs to us.

Night gushes down like a waterfall
and open hearts receive its freshness,
while remaining on the black
facades of the facing buildings
some lighted windows
where wakefulness is hope, impossible yielding
to sleep, a refusal and an attempt to prevail;
we will be thirsty all night,
turning our fevered bodies
until morning, while the heart
races at the overheard news
unable to pacify itself:
bird palpitating from its own song,
caged and restless from the morning
where the sumptuous and temporary red flower
unfurls, continuation of the thought,
clinging to the black and iron support
of the window,
flower at the threshold of vision that seizes
the first hours of the day
before entering into a renewed life;
constancy is the name of this flower nourished
with rain and gas, clinging
to the side, at the moment of passage,
lips that speak
of duration, despite
the fragile opening out and the certain wilting.

Trans. J.B. Anderson

LA COUPE OBSCURE

1 — Insouciance

Soir d'été, les dernières fleurs gonflent, se pressent.
Le ciel acide appelle un départ,
et les motos de mer jouent à faire des huit, des arabesques et
   des figures,
donnant forme au danger.
Le pont de Brooklyn devient guirlande,
sur la grisaille de la baie et des appontements.

Nous avions renoncé à nous asseoir
dans ce jardin, au cœur des immeubles,
inondé de l'eau des tourniquets,
où pourtant les enfants s'éclaboussaient en criant ;
tout proches, des téléphones publics, joyaux d'acier,
semblaient attendre la voix qui lie les êtres.

La mer, on ne la voyait pas ;
la nuit pénétrait nos paroles et les vagues renaissaient sans
   bruit.

THE DARK CUP

1 — Carelessness

Summer evening, the last flowers swell, crowd each other.
The acid sky calls for a departure,
and the motorboats play at making eights, forms and figures,
giving shape to danger.
The Brooklyn Bridge becomes a garland
on the greyness of the bay and the landing docks.

We had given up on sitting
in this garden, at the heart of the buildings,
inundated with water from the sprinklers,
where nonetheless children splashed crying out:
very close by, the public telephones, steel gems,
seemed to wait for the voice that links beings.

The sea—we did not see it;
night penetrated our words and the waves were reborn
    soundlessly.

2 — La coupe obscure

Ce fut à nouveau la joie, l'oubli.
Qui eût dit que nous buvions la coupe obscure,
que les pales, dans l'air, emportaient les mots,
doucement, la rosée devenait fleur dans la gorge,
la carte des étoiles se défaisait,
elles nous frappaient de leur froid
ou palpitaient, lointaines,
de l'éclat coupant qui crisse dans la mémoire.

La grève était maintenant délaissée de ses vagues,
de son vent ; la nuit pesait sur les maisons.

2 — The dark cup

That was renewed joy, oblivion.
Who would have said we were drinking the dark cup,
that the fan blades in the air were carrying off words,
gently, the dew became flower in the throat,
the map of the stars was unraveling,
they struck us with their coldness
or beat, at a distance,
with the cutting blow that scratches into memory.

The shoreline was now abandoned by its waves,
by its wind; night leaned on the houses.

3 — Travestissements

Revenir vers l'ombre des tilleuls
et le bruit du torrent, si loin désormais.
S'agit-il bien de cela ?

Faire un pas, avant la nuit,
yeux fixés sur
un maître disparu, redire sa parole,
y confronter ce jour ?

La teinte du rêve nuance l'automne.
Combien de fois revint cette saison !
Voici la gravure d'un intérieur
où nous fûmes autrefois, je la regarde,
accueillant le sentiment neuf,
mis en habit mythologique.

Nous redescendons vers des salles
souterraines, consacrées aux dieux anciens,
où le collectionneur a rassemblé
les formes de la croyance.
Le gardien évoque l'idée
de nous travestir l'un l'autre
des costumes
que nous aurions imaginés.
Mais, dans l'ombre, à l'angle de l'escalier,
un cri.

Un jour aussi, dans la prairie
aux tombes grises, nous lisions
leurs vers effacés ; il commençait à pleuvoir.

3 — Disguises

To return toward the shadow of the lindens
and the roar of the torrent, once so distant.
Is this really the question?

To take a step, before night,
eyes fixed on
a deceased master, to speak again his word,
confront it with this day?

The tint of dream nuances autumn.
How many times did this season return!
Here is the engraving of an interior
where we were once, I watch it,
greeting the new feeling,
cast in mythic clothing.

We go down again toward the rooms
underground, consecrated to ancient gods,
where the collector has gathered
the forms of belief.
The guardian evokes the idea
of us disguising one another
with the fancy dresses, the costumes
that we would have imagined.
But, in the shadow, at the angle of the staircase,
a cry.

One day also, in the prairie
of grey tombs, we read
their worn-away verses; the downpour began.

Trans. M. Kallet

TRISTES

1 — Une Grèce plus douce

Le regard traverse
le réel, pentes de la colline,
eau couleur
d'un ailleurs apaisé.
Des chemins s'ouvrent,
une fumée embrume le vert profond des pins,
bois odorants qu'on brûle,
leurs aiguilles tremblent sur le ciel tendre,
bleu ciel, bleu turquoise, bleu de plomb,
coupé d'ailes, écumant par vagues,
lumineux encore des immenses algues des mimosas qui se
    ploient.

Loin du monde,
où se perdent l'espace et le temps,
la pensée est libre ;
or, plus près de l'eau, je vois que les vagues se
pulvérisent sur les rochers :
le vertige
peut faire chanceler, le sentier côtier est dangereux.

Sur la route des collines,
les voitures laissent une traînée de diesel
dans le calme revenu.
Rencontres feutrées sur le parking ;
on n'évite pas longtemps le ballet des caddies entre les
    gondoles,
les sourires des femmes assises derrière les comptoirs en
    aluminium

TRISTIA

1 — A gentler Greece

The gaze traverses
the real, hillsides,
water color
of a calmed elsewhere.
Roads unfold,
a plume of smoke shrouds the deep green of pines,
fragrant timber for kindling,
their needles tremble against the tender sky,
blue sky, blue turquoise, lead blue,
sliced by wings, foaming by waves,
still luminous from the immense algae of mimosas that bend.

Far from everything,
where space and time lose themselves,
the mind is free;
then, nearer the water, I see that waves
pulverize themselves against rocks:
vertigo
can cause staggering, the coastal path is dangerous.

On the hillside road
cars leave a diesel trail
in the restored calm.
Muffled meetings on the parking lot;
one does not avoid for long the ballet of carts among the sets
    of shelves
the smiles of women seated behind the aluminum

et caoutchouc où glissent les achats,
le péristyle aux portes vitrées et coulissantes,
les échangeurs, dessinés comme pour se perdre
qui nous reconduisent à cet isolement factice,
ce fragile bonheur.

and rubber counters where the sales glide,
the peristyle with glass sliding doors
the interchanges, designed to get us lost
which escort us to this contrived isolation,
this fragile joy.

2 — Le Club 55

Le ciel et l'eau se séparent-ils ?
pas d'horizon, un violet diffus,
on passe à gauche
un sous-bois enchevêtré :
troncs noirs ou dorés, rouges,
touchés diversement par la lumière,
penchés, tordus, courts
— ils semblent parler.
Le contre-jour sur le pare-brise
rejette l'autre versant dans une douceur ancienne,
un nuage voile le dernier
soleil, d'une atonie lunaire,
ses ailes, très lentement,
explosent, se distendent dans une autre forme,
qui, submergée, se noie dans les lueurs tendres
de fin du jour.

— *Mais où est le Club 55 ?*
Un homme en noir, accompagné d'un chien
nous montre la plage de Pampelonne.
N'étions-nous pas
inquiets des beaux corps des baigneurs d'autrefois
dont les pas, entre les tamaris,
sont effacés ?

Nous revivons
la beauté d'hier,
en voiture, sur ces routes ondulantes
qui traversent un paysage creusé
de mille alvéoles dont les couleurs fondues
ne s'altèrent pas ;

2 — Club 55

Sky and water, do they separate?
no horizon, a diffuse violet,
on the left, one passes by
a tangled undergrowth:
black or gilded trunks, red ones,
touched diversely by the light,
bent, twisted, short,
—they seem to speak.
The lowlight on the windshield
rejects the other slope in an ancient gentleness,
a cloud veils the dying
sun, with a lunar atony,
its wings, very slowly
explode, distend into another form,
which, submerged, drowns in the tender glimmers
of dusk.

—*But where is Club 55?*
A man in black, accompanied by a dog
shows us the beach of Pampelonne.
Didn't we worry
about the beautiful bodies of the bathers of yore,
whose footsteps, between the tamarinds,
were washed away?

We relive
the beauty of yesterday,
in the car, on the undulant roads
which traverse a landscape hollowed
with thousands of honeycombs whose deep colors
do not alter;

les oiseaux persistent dans cette vie nouvelle.
Une voile
avance, entre l'eau
et le ciel, posée on ne sait où, venue du lointain
et du passé, elle risque une existence unique
et brillante, détachée,
malgré l'annonce de la pluie et tout
un coin de ciel menaçant.

Sublimes, les artefacts des stations-service,
des échangeurs : ces enseignes lumineuses,
ces réclames surréelles, auront bientôt,
dans la brume du soir, leur auréole floue.
Et, parmi l'arrangement sauvage des couleurs,
où nous risquons nos pas,
le battement de leur rayonnement intense
nous laissera captifs du hasard terrestre.

the birds persist in this new life.
A sail
approaches, between the water
and sky, set down one doesn't know where, come from afar
and from the past, it risks a singular
and gleaming existence, detached,
in spite of the sign of rain and all
a patch of sky menacing.

Sublimes, the artifacts of the gas stations,
of the interchanges, the luminous signage,
these surreal ads, will soon have
in the fog of evening, their hazy aureolae.
And, among the wild arrangement of colors,
where we risk our steps,
the pulsing of their intense radiance
will leave us captives of earthly chance.

Trans. M. Kallet

V

V

LOUXOR, PALAIS DU CINÉMA

Descendant l'avenue froide,
la foule pressée, houleuse,
piétine, trébuche sur le trottoir inégal,
glisse sur les déchets de toutes sortes,
arrêtée dans sa coulée par un mendiant unijambiste, un enfant
montrant ses bras difformes, une femme à fichu et lunettes
coffrée dans un sarcophage de cartons,
un vendeur de marrons, charbonneux
— odeur de mauvais combustible —
retournant ses trucs dans un réchaud calé sur un caddie ;
vitrines, parures de mariage
brillant, brillant
sur des mannequins de celluloïd aux poses d'un autre temps,
dentelles synthétiques de chemisiers en plein vent,
chaussures en vrac, de toutes tailles, sales d'être là,
pour quelle fille moderne aux goûts apprêtés ?

La pluie s'écoule dans la station rongée de rouille et patinée de
    crasse,
les pigeons y trouvent à ronger des trognons de maïs
ou des bouts de sandwich grec gras, sur des planches ;
entre des rambardes neuves,
trois hommes sont couchés, enveloppés,
nimbés d'une odeur étrange.
Attentes, le quai s'emplit de monde.
Le palais est là, derrière les vitres dépolies,
l'or de ses ornements hiéroglyphiques,
le jade et le turquoise
de sa mosaïque, revivent le soir,
et le palais abandonné se lève

LUXOR, MOVIE PALACE

Descending the cold avenue,
the hurrying crowd, swelling,
tramples, staggers on the uneven sidewalk,
slips on all sorts of trash,
stopped cold in its slide by a one-legged beggar, a child
displaying his withered arms, a woman in scarf and glasses
donning a sarcophagus of cardboard,
a chestnut vendor, smeared in charcoal
—smell of bad fuel—
turning his wares over and over on a portable stove mounted
    on a caddy;
plate glass windows, marriage finery
shining, shining
on celluloid models in yesterday's poses,
synthetic lace blouses fingered by the wind,
shoes in bulk, every size, dirty just from being there,
for what modern woman with borrowed tastes?

The rain pours into the station devoured by rust and clothed
    in filth,
the pigeons pick out nubs of corn to gnaw
or the ends of a greasy gyro, on the benches;
between the new guardrails,
three men sleep, tucked in,
haloed by a strange smell.
Expectations, the platform fills with people.
The palace is there, behind the frosted pane,
the gold of its hieroglyphic ornaments,
the jade and the turquoise
of its mosaic, revive in the evening,
and the abandoned palace rises

dans une ville aux carrefours enfin libres du trafic
et du tonnerre du métro qui arrive,
touché par la lumière à l'instant
où le reste s'abolit à contre-jour.

Le regard suit les rails, la perspective ;
dans la tranchée du ciel qu'ouvre le pont de fer de la ligne,
les nuages s'éclairent ;
des travailleurs se saluent ou se laissent
prendre par un demi-sommeil enfantin ;
bientôt, de nouveau sous terre dans la pénombre du boyau
grossièrement graphé,

Le chrome, c'est la couleur de l'arrache
La ville, c'est un truc
qui est fait pour être toujours cassé
On déchire les murs
pour faire pleurer les aveugles
Pour moi, le côté vandale, c'est la base du truc
Je me sens plus vandale
que rebelle. Je préfère la définition de vandale ;
les mecs qui lacèrent les sièges, qui cassent des vitrines
ça me fait délirer. Je trouve que ça va bien avec la société
    actuelle

nous filons, secoués et assourdis,
oubliant l'avènement d'un autre jour,
le mirage, le palais,
hier, le palais aux colonnettes d'albâtre
naissant de lotus épanouis
parmi les trottoirs encombrés d'étalages qui dégringolent,
de revendeurs de parfums ou de T-shirts.

in a city whose crossroads are at last free of traffic
and of the thunder of arriving trains,
touched by a ray at the moment
when everything else is extinguished by back lighting.

The look follows the rails, the perspective;
in the slice of light that the iron bridge of the railway opens,
clouds are illuminated;
workers greet each other or allow themselves
to be seized by a childish half-sleep;
soon, once more below the earth in the half-light of the bowels,
crudely drawn,

Chrome, the color of scratching, gouging,
the city is something
made to be broken
We tear up the walls
to make the blind cry
For me, vandalism's the thing
I feel more like a vandal
than a rebel. I prefer the definition of vandal;
the dudes who razor seats, break windows
make me bust a gut laughing. It goes well with the state of
   society

we flee, shaken up, deafened,
forgetting the arrival of another day,
the mirage, the palace,
yesterday, the palace with miniature alabaster columns
born from the flowering lotus
among the sidewalks crowded with cascading displays,
with perfume or t-shirt vendors.

Vers la Chapelle, Stalingrad,
le long des voies, des rails et des fils, se lèvent des paysages,
annoncés par les minces gazons des bordures, les balustrades
   de fer,
passerelles étroites et inaccessibles,
balisés des signaux étranges d'une contrée
hors des cartes,
et nous passons
devant les immeubles
murés, endommagés, effrités,
effondrés où s'avance le chantier qui abat,
éventre, montre
ce que les façades cachent encore : ces îlots
avec la fontaine et l'arbre,
abris et repos anachroniques,
les appentis aux toits bas,
la vie maladive, les squats, les logements aveugles,
les rues palissadées et lépreuses
où l'on dit que des enfants se vendent.

Le charbon de leurs yeux,
la menthe de leur souffle.

Towards la Chapelle, Stalingrad,
along the tracks, the rails and the wires, landscapes rise,
heralded by the thin edge of lawns, the balustrades of iron,
inaccessible and narrow footbridges,
marked by strange signals from a country
beyond maps,
and we pass
in front of walled-
up buildings, broken, crumbling,
collapsed where the construction site that knocks down,
eviscerates, shows
what facades still hide: these islands
with the fountain and the tree,
anachronistic refuge and repose,
the lean-tos with low roofs,
the diseased life, squatters, blind buildings,
the leprous and gated roads
where I have heard that children sell themselves.

The coal of their eyes,
The mint of their breath.

Trans. J.B. Anderson

LA DÉFENSE

Une esthétique seventies ?
Harmonie du gazon vert,
des costumes, magnolias,
couleurs écran d'ordinateur.
Utopie 2000
EDF, CCF, CNIT,
s'effacent derrière les ciels nuageux qu'ils portent —
    profondeur ?
Tours, séparées de vent invisible,
nos sandwiches aux raies colorées, dans
leur cellophane,
l'air, l'air sur les
passerelles, élévateurs, ascenseurs à l'odeur acide d'urine
niveaux 1, 2, zéro, moins 1.

Au loin, de la cendre du paysage, montent des fumées ;
mais ici, par places, des jardins, au croisement des voies
    express,
dans le bourdonnement, le soleil intense ;
sur la dalle,
l'homme au balai mécanique
attrape ce qui n'a pas été dispersé :
les miettes des repas en plein air,
leurs sachets transparents ;
dessous, on vit aussi :
livres, lunettes,
cigarettes ; des lettres :
M RER PARVIS
le nez stylisé d'un train,
pour ne pas se perdre
parmi les reflets

LA DÉFENSE

A Seventies aesthetic?
Harmony of green sod,
of wardrobes, magnolias,
computer screen colors.
Utopia 2000
EDF, CCF, CNIT,
are erased behind the cloudy skies that they carry—
    depth?
Towers, separated by invisible wind,
our sandwiches with colored stripes, in
their cellophane,
the air, the air on the
pathways, elevators, escalators with the acid odor of urine
level 1, 2, zero, minus 1.

In the distance, from the ash of the countryside, plumes of
    smoke rise;
but here, in places, gardens, at the crossing of express lanes,
in the drone, the intense sun;
on the flagstone,
the man with the mechanical sweeper
traps that which has not been dispersed:
the crumbs of meals in outdoor air,
their transparent sachets;
below, one also lives:
books, glasses,
cigarettes; letters:
M RER PARVIS
the stylized nose of a train,
in order to not get lost
among the reflections

des portes transparentes, hautes,
interdites ;
mais nous, avec nos écouteurs, pressés,
nous nous retranchons de ces allées
marmoréennes...

des files de voitures sont arrêtées, sous un soleil violent,
déjà 20.000 personnes sont parties en vacances...

remontons vers les allées granitiques ;
le rayon touche les baies noires
qu'on ne doit pas toucher, des sureaux en pots,
les baies qui grincent et luisent,
parmi ces détours grillagés
où l'été lance ses rameaux, entre deux falaises ;
sous les ponts, les bombages,
dans l'ombre s'affrontent : gueule, sinople, argent,
figures
de la Peur
et de la Faim qui tache la bouche et tord les membres.
Un peu de brume stagne au-dessus des maisons, dans la plaine
    vers
Saint-Germain-en-Laye.

of the transparent doors, high,
off-limits;
but we, with our earpieces, hurrying,
withdraw from these marbled
pathways...

the lines of cars have stopped, under a violent sun,
already 20,000 people have left on vacation...

we climb back toward the granitic pathways;
the sunbeam touches the blackberries
that one must not touch, the potted elders,
the berry bushes that creak and gleam
among the fenced detours
where summer hurls its branches, between two cliffs;
beneath the bridges, the sprayed graffiti,
in the shadow clash: gules, vert, argent,
faces
of Fear
and of Hunger that stains the mouth and twists the limbs.
A little fog stagnates below the houses, in the plain toward
Saint-Germain-en-Laye.

Trans. M. Kallet

UNE JOURNÉE, ICI

Dans les bruits du matin, sa fraîcheur, l'oiseau,
un courant d'air, le ronronnement lointain du passage des
    voitures,
les hauts murs qui nous entourent sont
rayés d'ombres, plaqués de lumière,
les corniches grises, dorées de soleil,
les falaises de meulière et de brique,
accrochées par la poussière, des esses
et le bleu du ciel bien haut, qui devient transparent,
réceptacle et réservoir
de la lumière,
le puits d'ombre des cours intérieures donné au vol des pigeons...
Écrans vastes le soir,
plages et falaises le matin,
sonneries, bruits de construction,
peut-être un marché qui se monte,
et dehors, les visages
étranges, les costumes étonnants des passants,
ce bouleversement du matin : la rencontre du visage adverse,
    des premiers cris
entendus, des alarmes sifflantes,
assourdies dans la chaleur d'une journée
qui sera belle,
un madrier chute, claquement d'une porte, bruit de pas, en
    dessous,
froissement de journaux,
désir d'ubiquité et, derrière ce matin-ci, celui d'une autre ville,
Londres. L'ombre s'est déplacée, c'est maintenant l'arête de
    l'immeuble
qui est couleur sable, le rose du revêtement s'illumine,

ONE DAY, HERE

In the noises of morning, its coolness, the bird,
a breeze, the distant hum of passing cars,
the high walls that surround us are
striped with shadows, plated with light,
the gray cornices, gilded by the sun,
the cliffs of millstone and brick
overhanging with dust, the hooks
and the blue of the sky high up, which becomes transparent,
receptacle and reservoir
of light,
the well of shadows in the interior courtyard lets the pigeons
    fly...
Vast screens in evening,
beaches and cliffs in morning,
doorbells, noises of construction,
perhaps a market setting up,
and outside, strange
faces, the surprising outfits of the passersby,
this disruption of morning: the meeting of the opposing face,
    the first cries
heard, the alarms shrilling,
muffled in the warmth of a day
that will be fair,
a beam falls, banging of a door, footsteps, below,
rustling of newspapers,
desire for ubiquity, and, behind this morning here, that of
    another city,
London. The shadow is displaced. It is now the bridge of the
    building
which is sand color, the pink of the surface lights it up,

les bords disparaissent, les coulées noirâtres forment un
    dessin, le grain particulier d'un
pan de mur prend un sens par contraste
et l'avion, les câbles en métal, le coup d'aile, le moteur
indiquent des directions, tandis qu'une porte claque,
aboiement d'un petit chien,
paroles rapides en chinois,
c'est avant de prononcer une parole,
d'ouvrir un livre, papiers froissés, plastiques, plus proches,
un moteur démarre et s'arrête,
le chien aboie de nouveau ;
puis le soleil se cache.

Mais au fond de la mélancolie,
la source silencieuse ride la surface de l'eau.
De façon presque imperceptible,
minuscule, un courant se fait
et tend à emporter les feuilles sèches, les pétales tombés,
et promettre une nouvelle floraison.
Voici les visages, la floraison des
robes, ce samedi, sur le boulevard,
l'activité, la densité, la bousculade
des pieds, des pieds nus dans des sandales, auxquels un lacet
    fin
accroche une marguerite en plastique stylisée qui luit,
les cris, le désordre, fait de l'entrecroisement de toutes ces
    routes
barrées par des gens immobiles
et ces visages, gais, nerveux, inquiets,
crispés, provocateurs, menaçants,
perdus, aperçus vite. Et puis,
dans l'indistinction houleuse des couleurs

the shores disappear, the blackish drippings form a design, the
    particular grain
of a patch of wall takes on meaning by contrast
and the plane, the metal cables, the smack of a wing, the motor
indicate directions, while a door bangs,
barking of a little dog,
rapid words in Chinese,
this is before pronouncing a word,
opening a book, papers rustling, plastics, nearer,
a motor starts up and stops,
the dog barks again;
then the sun hides itself.

But in the depths of melancholy,
the silent source ripples the surface of the water.
In an almost imperceptible manner,
minuscule, a current stirs
and tends to carry off the dry leaves, the fallen petals,
and promises a new flowering.
Here are the faces, the flowering
of dresses, this Saturday, on the boulevard,
the activity, the density, the jostling
of feet, the feet bare in sandals, to which a thin lace
attaches a stylized plastic daisy that shines,
the cries, the disorder, made of the intersection of all these
    paths
blocked by people standing still,
and the faces, cheerful, nervous, worried,
clenched, provocative, menacing,
lost, noticed quickly. And then,
in the cloudy indistinction of the colors

et la signification impossible à fixer,
les boutiques odorantes s'ouvrent comme des jardins,
au loin, le métro passe sur le pont aérien,
les feux rouges sont inutiles et les voitures qui bouchent toute
    l'avenue
n'avancent plus,
des boissons dans des seaux de glace qu'on propose à 1€,
des prix, des occases,
et ces froissements de chaque instant, les paroles
et les bruits de différents registres,
saisis par instant et reconnaissables alors
dans leur incomplétude, leur fragmentation,
comme une vague de la grande rumeur
vaine, cette démonstration de vie est joyeuse, la voir répare
    tout,
diversité heureuse, c'est la végétation qui renaît sur la rive
    calcinée,
la forme se refait, dans la soif d'être, de connaître,
ce qui luit au fond des yeux, ce qui vient au-devant de nous,
bouches toutes différentes, d'où sortent des paroles
et la bouche d'eau figure la fontaine de cette place villageoise
rêvée, autour y restent tout le jour la vieille femme qui
    quémande
sur sa chaise et le vendeur du bazar d'à côté
qui y rince le verre de thé, s'y rafraîchit les pieds,
et quelques touristes, égarés dans cette zone,
déploient leur plan de Paris.
Plus tard, dans la nuit, ce seront les hordes de malheureux,
avec leurs hurlements,
zigzaguant, hululant
sur le trottoir, oscillants, penchés vers le caniveau.

and the significance impossible to decide,
aromatic boutiques open like gardens,
in the distance, the metro passes on the overhead bridge,
the red lights are useless and cars that clog the whole avenue
do not move,
the drinks in the buckets of ice that are offered for 1 €,
the prices, the bargains,
and these rustlings of each instant, the words
and the noises of different registers,
seized by the instant and recognizable then
in their incompleteness, their fragmentation,
like a wave of the great vain
uproar, this demonstration of life is joyous, to see it repairs
    everything,
joyful diversity, it's the vegetation that is reborn on the
    calcined riverbank,
form reshapes itself, in the thirst for being, for knowing,
that which gleams in the depths of eyes, that which comes
    ahead of us,
mouths all different, from which words come forth
and the spout of water shapes the fountain of this village
    square
dreamed, around it stay the old woman all day who begs
on her chair and the bazaar vendor alongside
who rinses his tea glass, cools his feet,
and some tourists, straying into this zone,
unfold their maps of Paris.
Later, in the night, there will be gangs of the miserable,
with their howling,
zigzagging, hooting
on the sidewalk, swaying, leaning toward the gutter.

Mélancolie de cette perte,
dans les sirènes qui tournent par les rues
alentour et les nuages plus noirs que
la nuit qui tendent à recouvrir les parcelles
de ciel découpées par les toits,
un orage s'annonce,
les cris du soir dans les cours voisines
et ces bourrasques d'un vent plus froid
qui menacent de tout renverser,
un disque joue de l'orgue électrique,
aux sonorités rondes et dorées,
comme venues d'entrailles chaudes,
ce sont les cris artificiels du jeu et son rythme irriguant les
    corps
qui dessinent l'arborescence intérieure, comme
travaillée à l'eau-forte, les pigeons sont encore à roucouler
sur l'étai de fer, un avion passe,
l'attention se creuse, tout échappe,
un bruit d'ailes, la rumeur est atténuée,
il pleut maintenant et ce bruit couvre tout,
on ferme des fenêtres, la pluie augmente.

Melancholia of this loss,
in the sirens that turn through the surrounding
streets and the clouds blacker than
the night that stretch to recover the parcels
of skies carved by the roofs,
a storm brews,
the cries of the evening in the neighboring courtyards
and these gusts of a colder wind
that threaten to turn everything upside down,
a disc plays some electric organ,
with rounded and golden tones,
as if issued from warm entrails,
these are the artificial cries of the game and its rhythm
    irrigating bodies
that design interior arborescence, as if
worked into etching, the pigeons are still cooing
on the steel stays, a plane passes by,
the attention tires, everything escapes,
a noise of wings, the rumor is attenuated,
it rains now and this noise covers everything,
windows are shut, the rain increases.

Trans. M. Kallet

LA CHAMBRE NUPTIALE DE L'HÔTEL MODERNE

Sous ces nuages, amas de neige rose,
synthétique,
la mer découvre, à contre-jour,
comme un dos de baleine, une banquise, dérivant,
se défaisant dans l'eau.
La promenade au bord de la grève, mène sous les fenêtres de
la chambre nuptiale de l'Hôtel Moderne.
Sonne un portable :
« — Alors, tu…
— oui, moi aussi… » ;
sous la ciselure vibrante du clocher, les cloches raniment les
    fleurs
gaies des tombes défiant le pourrissement, cet enfoncement
    dans le sable,
gorgé d'eau de mer, des corps des morts.

De quelle couleur seront les poissons
pêchés dans le bras qui nous sépare de l'autre rive,
où les pêcheurs, violets, immobiles, avancés dans l'eau
jusqu'aux genoux, ont lancé leurs lignes ;
les poissons de cette eau rose, mauve et bleu pétrole irisée ?

Cependant les drapeaux **Bouygues Télécom** flottent
    doucement
au souffle du soir ; et les pensionnaires de l'hôtel sont attablés
derrière la vitre qui reçoit le coucher de soleil en face ; le taxi
rentre à son poste et nous croisons un solitaire

THE BRIDAL CHAMBER OF THE
HOTEL MODERNE

Below the clouds, heap of pink snow,
synthetic,
the sea, like the back of a whale, reveals
against the light
an ice floe, drifting,
breaking apart in the water.
The promenade at the edge of the shore leads below the
    windows of
the bridal chamber at the Hotel Moderne.
A mobile phone rings:
"—So, you…"
"—yes, me too…";
below the vibrant engraving of the steeple, the bells reawaken
    the cheerful flowers
of tombs defying decay, this hollow in the sand
gorged with sea water, with the bodies of the dead.

What color will the fish be
caught in the sound that separates us from the other shore,
where the fishermen, violet, still, ahead in the water
up to their knees, have cast their lines;
the fish of this pink water, mauve and blue iridescent gasoline?

Meanwhile the flags **Bouygues Télécom** float gently
on the breath of evening; and the boarders at the hotel are at
    tables
behind the pane glass which gets the evening sun head on; the
    taxi
resumes its post as we cross a solitary man

devant le panneau jaune **MOULES-FRITES** *en terrasse* ; tous
   les réchauds éteints,
il flotte encore une odeur de friture,
le distributeur bancaire clignote dans le jour qui baisse,
un graffiti noir mal recouvert de blanc crie
LA PECHE CRÈVE ; après le buisson de fuchsia,
nous longeons l'église et le mur du cimetière,
une idée plus fraîche de demain nous saisit.

in front of the yellow billboard **MUSSELS AND FRIES** *on the*
   terrace; all chafing dishes
extinguished,
still an odor of fried food wafts,
the bank ATM flashes in the fading daylight,
black graffiti badly covered with white screams
FISHERY DIES; after the fuchsia bush
we go along the church and the wall of the cemetery,
a fresher idea of tomorrow overtakes us.

Trans. M. Kallet

DÉSAFFECTÉ

Aux abords de la ville, entre les zones urbanisées
et d'anciens quartiers à l'abandon,
des vergers sauvages,
des arbres fruitiers porteurs de promesses,
parmi les ronces, des mûriers, passant les petits murs,
une cour de ferme d'autrefois
qu'on devine encore, face maintenant à un hangar en béton
    fermé d'une porte coulissante de tôle verte,
quelqu'un a arrangé là un jardin —
et, de l'autre côté de l'ancienne buvette à l'enseigne rouillée,
    salle basse où l'on accédait en descendant trois marches,
rouillée, illisible,
après avoir traversé, une ancienne usine
aux bouches de lumière arrondies, ses fortes poutres
    métalliques,
sa vaste cour intérieure carcérale, changée en
« lieu unique » offert à la dérive des jeunes d'aujourd'hui,
devenu habité, déplaçant ainsi les rêves de la
petite ville vers ces rues naguère désertées ;
je ne savais pourquoi je prenais le chemin de cette usine
    désaffectée
après avoir contourné la Maison Pour Tous
par ses massifs ordonnés autour d'une vaste salle,
peut-être un réfectoire, dont on avait encombré les tables de
    caisses de livres,
de rebuts, on dirait que les marchands sont déjà passés,
il n'y a plus grand chose d'intéressant : *Les Mystères de
    Londres,*
un Francis Carco, un Gallimard blanc de Jean Follain, *Canisy* :
    ses souvenirs d'enfance, quelques pages très écrites,
    émouvantes, au fond, un portemanteau

DISUSED

At the city limits, between the urbanized zones
and the old districts left abandoned,
wild orchards,
fruit trees bearers of promises,
among the brambles, blackberry bushes overgrowing the walls,
a former farmyard
that one can still discern, now faces a concrete shed closed
   with a sliding
door in green sheet metal,
someone arranged a garden there—
and, from the other side of the ancient taproom with the
   rusted sign, lower deck where one
gained access by going down three steps
rusted, unreadable,
after having crossed, a former factory
with rounded openings for light, its strong metal beams,
its vast interior carceral courtyard, changed into
"unique venue" offered for drifting to the youth of today
now inhabited, thus displacing the dreams of the
little city toward these streets not so long ago deserted;
I did not know why I took the path of this disused factory
after having bypassed the House For All
by its piles arranged around a vast room,
perhaps a refectory, on which crates of books had been
   heaped up on tables,
discards, one might say that the booksellers had already
   passed over,
there's no longer much of interest: *Les Mystères de Londres,*
a Francis Carco, a white Gallimard by Jean Follain, *Canisy*:
   his memoirs of childhood, some very composed pages,
   moving, in the depths, a coat rack

avec des vêtements de seconde main, le contenu des caisses est
   assez homogène,
livre pieux, livres pop, livres d'intérêt historique, certains
   recouverts d'un papier identique, provenant d'une même
   bibliothèque, leur ancien possesseur les a numérotés, et
   marqués du nom de l'auteur, au dos, ceux-là
sont bien rangés dans les caisses, n'ont aucun intérêt,
dehors, sur une pelouse au soleil, des enfants jouent à chat,
   des femmes discutent,
dès neuf heures, les gens se pressaient, on a été obligés d'ouvrir
à dix heures moins le quart, les gens se bousculaient pour
   entrer, oui,
pour votre mère, ça dépend, vous pouvez lui offrir des
   Harlequin, des histoires d'amour, il y a des personnes âgées
   qui lisent ça, pour les personnes âgées, c'est plus facile.
— oui, c'est ça, c'est plus facile…
— mais ça dépend si votre mère est cultivée, y a des personnes
   âgées qui achètent même des livres pour enfants et qui lisent
   ça, oui.
— oui, ça dépend…
— vous voulez un sac en plastique, j'en ai ramené de chez moi
   parce que je pensais bien qu'y en aurait pas.
La femme avait raison,
l'homme-enfant n'a finalement pas choisi de livre pour sa mère.
Derrière, dans d'autres pièces obscures pleines d'objets pêle-
   mêle,
bouilloires, tasses, chaussures en vrac, paniers,
de couleurs et de matières curieuses,
parfois en parfait état,
des femmes dans la pénombre se racontaient la vie,
fouillant lentement parmi les déballages d'Emmaüs.

with secondhand clothing, the contents of the crates are fairly
   homogeneous,
pious books, pop books, books of historical interest, certain
   ones recovered with an identical paper, provenance of the
   same library, their former possessor had
numbered them, and marked with the name of the author, on
   the back, those there
are well-arranged in the cases, are of no interest,
outside, on a lawn in sun the children play tag, the women talk,
since 9 a.m. the people began to crowd, we were obliged to
   open up at 9:45, the people jostled each other to get in, yes,
for your mother, that depends, you can offer her the
   Harlequins, the stories of love, there are older people who
   read that, for the older people, it's easier.
"—yes, that's it, easier."
"—but that depends if your mother is well-read, there're
   older people who even buy books for children and who
   read them, yes."
"—yes, it depends…"
"—you want a plastic bag, I brought some from home
   because I thought surely they might not have any."
The woman was right,
the man-child did not in the end choose a book for his mother.
Behind, in other dark rooms full of objects pell-mell,
kettles, cups, random shoes, baskets,
of colors and of odd materials,
sometimes in perfect shape,
women in the shadows talked about life,
rummaging slowly among the unpackings of Emmaus.

Trans. M. Kallet

OUISTREHAM OU CYTHÈRE

Plage large, flanquée de bâtiments de béton blancs,
de baraquements de boissons, de glaces ;
plus loin, c'est bien un tableau de Boudin,
mais avec, au premier plan, de gigantesques potences
où les enfants se pendent en riant, à l'élastique ;
trait net, couleurs contrastées, allongement
de l'horizon, un peu haut ; et cet envahissement du bleu,
le sable beige foncé largement détrempé de flaques de ciel et
    ces nuages passant,
porteurs de vastes figures et ourlées d'ombres orageuses,
l'eau, très loin, dont on aperçoit à peine
les vagues ;
le bunker, converti en musée, repeint à neuf,
les vacanciers, déambulant dans la rue principale,
mangeant des glaces, des beignets,
dans une atmosphère infusée du parfum doux des gaufres
et des barbes à papa,
contents.
La rue perpendiculaire à la mer,
sur laquelle se sont plaqués les commerces nécessaires
à notre bonheur estival, la rue piétonne,
avec ses maisons de la presse, ses carteries,
banques, terrasses ; on aperçoit à peine,
entre les avancées des étalages,
les stores des vitrines, les tourniquets,
dans les renfoncements, des jardins étroits
et de petites maisons, anciennes villégiatures,
parmi les rosiers buissonnants, à l'ombre ;

OUISTREHAM OR CYTHERA

Large beach, flanked by buildings of white concrete,
by shelters for drinks, for ice cream,
farther off, it's very much a painting by Boudin,
but with enormous gallows in the foreground
where the children hang laughing from the bungee;
clean line, contrasting colors, lengthening
of the horizon, a bit high: and this invasion of blue,
the beige sand deepened largely saturated with pools of sky
   and these passing clouds,
bearers of vast faces and hems of stormy shadows,
water, very far off, on which one hardly notices
the waves:
the bunker, converted into a museum, repainted anew,
the vacationers, wandering down the main street,
eating ice cream, donuts,
in an atmosphere infused with gentle perfume from waffles
and cotton candy,
content.
The street perpendicular to the sea,
on which are plastered the necessary commercials
for our summer happiness, the pedestrian street
with its newsstands, its sellers of postcards,
benches, terraces; one hardly notices,
among the overhanging displays,
the awnings of the store windows, the turnstiles,
in the doorways of the narrow gardens
and of little houses, former resorts,
among the rose bushes, in the shadow;

oubliées, elles portent les détails désuets
qui permettaient de les distinguer autrefois :
trois carreaux de faïence
au coin d'une fenêtre.

forgotten, they bear the quaint details
that allowed one to detect them in the old days:
three earthenware tiles
in the corner of a window.

Trans. M. Kallet

NAVIGATION

Nous tournons autour du cargo ;
trois hommes sur le pont : deux lavent, un troisième passe et
    fait un signe ;
MILANO
NASSAU
tout blanc et allégé, bien au-dessus de l'eau, il attend, drapeau
    rouge, blanc et vert
et or,
plus près, une odeur de fuel et de rouille ; fumée,
nostalgie des orages ;
le poisson pris se débat dans le seau,
l'éclabousse du sang qu'il perd par les ouïes.
Et voici la plage jaune, oxydée,
le quai cyclopéen.

NAVIGATION

We turn around the cargo;
three men on the bridge: two are scrubbing, a third passes by
  and gives a sign;
MILANO
NASSAU
all white and lighter, well above water, it waits, red, green and
  white
and gold flag,
nearer, an odor of fuel and of rust; smoke,
nostalgia for storms;
the caught fish thrashes in the bucket,
splatters blood that oozes from its gills.
And here is the yellow beach, oxidized,
the Cyclopean pier.

Trans. M. Kallet

ORIGINE

Je lève les yeux : la lune est là, très transparente et fine,
comme nouvelle, juste en face

errance

... mangez ctml, pour une meilleure gestion
de votre capital santé...

trop de choix, et pourtant, l'œil exercé
élimine des rayons entiers inchoisissables,
l'amabilité
des personnes, entre les gondoles
où l'on déambule,
légumes propres,
fruits qui ont perdu leurs feuilles, ou avec leurs feuilles, plus
   rassurants ainsi,
télés
où le Conseil Régional diffuse des films d'époques révolues,
propose une fidélité réciproque,
les sacs en plastique,
recyclables, portent une photo très ressemblante de la Nature,
à la maison,
les fruits dé-durcissent,
dans le compotier, ont l'air d'avoir
été cueillis dans le verger,
radio en bruit blanc :

... il descend de son jet privé
en simple chemisette bleue...

ORIGIN

I look up: the moon is there, very transparent and thin,
like new, right in front

wandering

...eat ctml, for better management
of your health...

too much choice, and nevertheless, the trained eye
eliminates entire unselectable rays
the likeability
of people, between the shelves
where one wanders,
clean vegetables,
fruits that have lost their leaves, or with leaves, thus more
    reassuring,
TVs
where the Regional Council broadcasts films of times gone by,
suggests a mutual loyalty,
plastic bags,
recyclables, carrying a photo that holds a strong likeness to
    Nature,
back home,
fruits un-harden
in the compote bowl, have the appearance of having
been picked in the orchard,
radio in white noise:

...he stepped out of his private jet
in a simple short-sleeved shirt...

... continuer
les attentats-suicides...

Le soir embellit et adoucit toutes choses,
redonne aux fruits leur poids.

...to continue
the suicide attacks...

The evening embellishes and softens all things,
gives back to the fruits their weight.

Trans. M. Kallet

CÉLÉBRATION

Des fleurs explosent,
des étoiles, des serpents de mer, des méduses,
se haussent,
fleurissent pour vomir leur être,
disperser leur forme,
leur couleur,
n'être plus, après l'élan, que tige de fumée
retombée dans l'eau violacée de la baie.
Bonshommes, monstres, pailletés d'or,
l'un après l'autre,
jaillissent, s'évanouissent...
les enfants avec, à la main, leurs lampions de papier,
    regardent, bouche bée ;
et la lune ronde est au-dessus des bois noirs.

Au cœur des Affinités électives, souviens-toi,
il y a ce feu d'artifice qu'on donne, au bord du lac,
pour le peuple, massé sur l'autre rive ;
bruit sans autre blessure que l'étonnement,
son écho en photo :
le pont de Brooklyn,
ainsi whistlérien, dans la nuit d'été,
ou dans l'hiver, à la lumière diurne,
sur cette autre photo,
le miroir de la baie, du lac, d'une autre baie ;
célébration,
conjuration des guerres, évocation d'ombres
évanouies, un instant.

CELEBRATION

Flowers explode,
stars, sea serpents, Medusas,
rise up,
flower to purge their being,
disperse their form,
their color,
to be, after the elation, no more than stem of smoke
refallen in the violet-blue water of the bay.
Goodfellows, monsters, with flakes of gold,
one after another,
surge, disappear...
children with their paper lanterns in hand, look, gaping;
et la lune ronde est au-dessus des bois noirs.

At the heart of Elective Affinities, remember,
there are these fireworks that one offers at the lake's edge,
for people massed on the other shore,
noise without other wound than astonishment,
its echo in photo:
the Brooklyn Bridge,
Whistlerian in the summer night,
or in the winter, by the diurnal light
on this other photo,
the mirror of the bay, the lake, another bay;
celebration,
conjuring of wars, evocation of shadows
vanishing, a moment.

Trans. M. Kallet

DANS LA NUIT

Rien, dans la nuit,
que ce ruban électrique
qui dessine la côte ;
une ville, de loin en loin, se marque d'un monceau brillant
et ce clignotement
appelle à être aussi ailleurs,
atome d'une autre beauté brasillante ;

nuit de la mer, nuit du sable,
on ne voit plus la vague mais on entend
ce bruit ;
là-bas,
un arc noir, qui est la terre, se cerne d'une phosphorescence ;
la nuit n'est pas tout à fait refermée sur l'étendue ;

bientôt, les lumières battent d'une existence incertaine,
tracent le contour du rivage ;
et, entre ici et là-bas, la nuit close,
se pare de la guirlande des vies, maintenant visibles
et tremblantes.

INTO THE NIGHT

Nothing tonight but
this electric ribbon
tracing the coastline;
here and there a city appears a shining heap
and this twinkling
calls for being elsewhere,
atom of another incandescent beauty;

sea night, sand night,
we can't see the waves anymore but we can hear
this noise;
over there,
a black curve, which is land, ringed in phosphorescence;
the night is not completely pinned to the horizon;

soon, the lights pulse with an uncertain existence,
outlining the contours of the shoreline;
and, between here and there, the night falls,
garlanded with lives, now visible
and trembling.

Trans. J.B. Anderson

ANCRAGE

Un paysage paraît,
reposant, vaste et peut-être infini, au-delà des collines…

Ces collines, sont aussi celles du souvenir,
baignées du soleil fort ; et les reparcourir aujourd'hui,
atténuées et musicales, révèle cet ancrage,
rehausse leur dessin d'un vent frais, les pénètre de fragilité.

Et l'on va, en esprit, parmi le bonheur de drapeaux colorés
qui claquent tout autour ;
entêtés dans cette confrontation
où le dialogue se construit.

Des routes marquent ce paysage
dont *l'infini* n'est qu'impression fugitive,
dissipée dans la clarté et le jeu
du tissage des mots,
entre hier et maintenant, dans cette répétition,
ce martèlement inquiet du réel.

MOORINGS

A landscape appears,
restful, vast and perhaps infinite, over the hills…

These hills, which also belong to memory,
bathed in glaring sunlight; and crisscrossing them today,
softened and musical, reveals this anchorage,
lifts their contours with a fresh breeze, penetrates them with
    weakness.

And we go, in spirit, among the happy colored flags
that flap all about;
entrenched in struggle
where dialogue builds up.

Roads mark this landscape
where the *infinite* is only a passing sensation,
dissolved in the glare and this game
this weaving of words,
between yesterday and now, in this repetition,
this unsettling hammering of the real.

Trans. J.B. Anderson

ÉCLORE

Cette fleur inconnue qui trouble,
masque miniature
de mort, objet opaque,
tu t'en es détourné, ne pouvant défaire
les chaînes muettes.

La teinte et la texture de cette floraison brusque…
il faut maintenant
éblouir le ciel noir de sa révélation
puisque son oubli porterait la mort
solitaire et nue.

Elle éclora ainsi, autre étoile,
écarlate et sans feu ;
et le lent basculement du ciel,
dans la régularité de son mouvement,
niera l'élan de sa couleur
pour tisser, à la manière d'un destin,
l'espace où tu vis ;
sur la même tige qui lie terre et ciel
s'attachent la peine
et le vertige.

Les étoiles, la voie lactée, deux avions clignotent.

BLOOM

This unknown flower that disturbs,
miniature mask
of death, opaque object,
you turned away from it, not able to undo
the mute chains.

The hue and the texture of this abrupt flowering…
it must now
dazzle black sky with its revelation
since its oblivion would carry death
solitary and bare.

It will blossom like this, another star,
scarlet and without fire;
and the slow swinging of the sky,
in the regularity of its movement,
will negate the verve of its color
to weave, in the style of a destiny,
the space where you live;
on the same stalk that ties earth and sky
pain
and vertigo cling.

The stars, the Milky Way, two planes glimmer.

Trans. M. Kallet

PANORAMA

Un long moment, le panorama,
si variable ici,
sembla se figer, des nuages congelés
se maintenaient à la même hauteur de l'horizon marin
au-dessus d'une bande d'un jaune-vert opalin,
l'air était tout à fait calme ;
et, quelques heures après, la mer fut
bleu électrique, comme artificiel,
d'un bleu profond de pierre, remué
par la passion des yeux qui y noient leur désir,
et aussi, par places, d'un gris
atone de miroir uni.
Tout nuage avait disparu ;
ainsi, en quelques minutes, l'aperçu pouvait changer,
et ce qui paraissait immuable
étendait maintenant à l'horizon
des accords jusque-là inconnus.

C'est encore la pensée de la séparation
qui isole parmi la foule désœuvrée,
en quête de désennui,
de barbes à papa, de soldes ;
nous allons, anesthésiés,
au sein de cette lente déambulation sur fond sonore,
de foire estivale,
au cœur méconnaissable de la splendeur ancienne,
dans le bercement des paroles,
et l'hébétement doux, dans nos yeux,
des visages passant...

PANORAMA

For a long moment the panorama,
so changeable here,
seemed to freeze, icy clouds
hovered above the ocean's horizon
over an opalescent yellow-green band,
the air was completely calm;
and, some hours later, the sea was
electric blue, almost fake,
a deep stony blue, troubled
by passionate eyes drowning their desire within,
and also, in places, the drab
grey of plain mirrors.
Every cloud had disappeared;
thus, in a matter of minutes, perception could change,
and what seemed unchanging
now spread harmonies unknown until that moment
all the way to the horizon.

It is still the thought of separation
that isolates within the restless crowd
seeking distraction
in cotton candy and sales;
we go, anesthetized,
in the midst of this slow and echoing shuffle
of this summer fair,
to the unrecognizable heart of the old splendor,
cradled by voices,
and the sweet stupor, in our gaze,
of the passing faces...

Trans. J.B. Anderson

EN CETTE SAISON

IN THIS SEASON

OMBRES CHIFFRÉES

1 —

Le tablier de la cheminée porte ces taches de rouille,
ombres chiffrées, personnages chinois,
au bord du fleuve. Ils agitent des fanions
dans le ciel noir, l'air pailleté de signes ;
l'un porte un morion,
une baguette à pommeau rond,
son geste en impose,
il nous regarde, mais se tient à genoux
et ses jambes, pliées sous lui, sont de profil.
À cet instant, éclair d'artifice sur la nuit :
minces silhouettes
qui, de loin, le saluent ;
une foule indistincte, à droite,
— un bosquet, aussi bien —
immobile, attend un mot pour s'avancer.

Sur les deux bandes inférieures,
sont un tournoi,
dans le désordre arrangé de ses piétinements et, en bas,
un ouragan qui s'abat sur le rivage.

SHADOW CIPHERS

1 —

The fireplace blower bears rust stains,
shadow ciphers, Chinese personae
at the edge of a river. They shake pennants
in the black sky, the air sequined with signs;
one wears a morion,
a rod with round pommel,
his gesture imposing
he watches us, but remains kneeling
and his legs, folded under him, are in profile.
In this instant, burst of firework on night:
thin silhouettes
who, from afar, salute him;
an indistinct mob, to the right
—a grove, as well—
immobile, waits the word to advance.

On the two lower bands
is a tournament,
in the ordered mess of its shufflings and, below,
a hurricane breaking over the coast.

2 —

L'été a sombré :
couchers de soleil
turquoise sur les lacs intouchés,
barres de tyrien,
s'exhaussent
du mauve floconneux où tout avait
commencé. « — Plus que quelques
minutes », dit le haut-parleur :
il faut rejoindre le parking.
Ce lac et ses rives
avaient l'air d'une promenade aménagée,
le sombre des pins s'écarta
et l'eau, en contrebas, sa nacre,
sa sauvagerie
parurent.

2 —

Summer sank:
sunsets
turquoise on the untouched lakes,
magenta bars,
rise
from the mauve little flakes where all had
begun. "—Several more
minutes," said the loudspeaker:
time to return to the parking lot.
This lake and its banks
had the feel of an arranged promenade
the gloom of the pines parted
and the water, below, its mother-of-pearl,
its savagery
appeared.

3 —

Atteindrions-nous là-bas,
portés par l'accolade des vagues,
une fois traversé le flot, brouillé des pluies
qui ne cessent pas, en cette saison,
et forcé le recul de l'inconnu ;
est-ce déjà trop loin ?
Voir noir, ne plus voir ;
chaque instant, paralysé,
assister à la naissance désordonnée
de quelque chose.
Une virée en taxi devient cet instant sombre.
La pluie avait détrempé mes vêtements,
le parcours s'accomplissait,
dans la ville encombrée, à midi.

3 —

Were we to reach there at last,
carried by the accolade of waves,
once across the tide befuddled by rain
that does not stop, in this season,
and forced the retreat of the unknown;
is it already too far?
To see black, to see no more;
each instant, paralyzed,
to assist the uncoordinated birth
of something.
A taxi joyride becomes this somber moment.
The rain had soaked my clothes,
the route completed,
in the cluttered city, at noon.

4 —

Signes, paroles,
réverbérations polaires
sur des espaces non franchis,
franchis,
intouchables,
touchés, fleurs, fleurs
sur l'eau reflétées, accrochées
aux branches.
Avancée.
Comme un chant de rivière,
ce ciel de palais montagneux,
le noir des forêts alpestres,
tout ce chant.
Aube non blanche, mais orange intense
gonflant derrière les falaises atones
des immeubles qui s'écartent,
pour l'embrasement, avant le jour.
Lorsque passe le Néant…
Être fragile
qui trembles
et ne peux espérer
enfin que ce qui EST,
dans la réconciliation, peut-être,
d'une pensée continuée.

4 —

Signs, words
polar reverberations
in the uncrossed spaces,
crossed,
untouchable,
touched, flowers, flowers
on the glistening water, caught
in the branches.
Advanced.
Like a river-song,
this mountainous palace of sky,
the dark of alpine forests,
all this song.
Dawn not white, but intense orange
swelling behind the lifeless cliffs
of buildings that part,
for the blaze, before day.
When passes the Nothing...
Fragile being
you who tremble
and can hope
at last only this that IS,
in the reconciliation, maybe,
of a thought continued.

5 —

Au froid, se forme
une étoile,
et l'arrangement de ses branches
danse ;
lui répondent le vent et le souffle
des bêtes apprivoisées,
le crissement électrique de la pensée
dans le temps —
ô tout ce qui manque
et qui est perdu.
Comment cela s'est-il fait ?
Pendant que la lune tourne,
éclairant les affiches,
on entend des cris,
on s'est éloigné des bêtes,
de la lune, écume, neige, étoile...

5 —

In the cold, it forms itself
a star,
and the arrangement of its branches
dances;
answering it, the wind and breath
of tamed beasts,
the electric screech of thought
in time —
O all that is missing
and that is lost.
How is it done?
While the moon turns,
lighting posters,
one hears shouts,
one moves away from the beasts,
from the moon, foam, snow, star...

6 —

Le tablier de la cheminée tremble ;
dehors, le froid brûle
et, dans la nuit, notre nuit, sachant que
ce sont les derniers instants :
descente en ascenseur,
soupir profond
de tristesse ;
cet homme entre,
avec sa poubelle à roulettes et son balai,
douleur à la pliure
d'un monde — visage
en pleurs —
où les choses sont posées comme
obstacles.

6 —

The fireplace blower trembles;
outside, the cold burns
and, in the night, our night, knowing that
these are the last moments:
descent in elevator,
deep sigh
of sadness;
that man enters
with his wheeled trashcan and his broom,
pain in the folds
of a world—face
in tears—
where things are posed like
obstacles.

7

Par les trouées des nuages
congelés et neigeux qui déployaient leur rythme,
un autre panorama filait,
sous un ciel dégagé,
de ceux qui touchent les cimes ;

dans l'intervalle, une lumière irregardable
sur les bords de cette ouverture
et nous n'étions déjà plus là,
sur terre, mais dans un paysage, ailleurs ;
seuls les mots *beau, belle nature*
pouvaient être dits
et nous regagnâmes la maison :
l'ombre avançait et
les formes
passaient, engendrant
maintenant des étendues roses
qui n'avaient plus rien
d'ici.

7 —

By the gaps in the frozen
and snowy clouds deploying their rhythm
another panorama flew by
under a clear sky
of those who touch the peaks;

in the interval, an unviewable light
on the edges of this opening
and already we were no longer there
on earth, but in a countryside, elsewhere;
only the words *beautiful, beautiful nature*
could be said
and we returned home:
the shadow advanced and
the forms
happened, engendering
now rose expanses
that no longer had anything
of here.

8

Quelques fleurs, imprimées sur fond noir,
peuvent concentrer une image passée,
et ce parfum qu'elle n'ont pas
s'échapper de leur dessin ;
en ce moment où je les regarde,
se serrent les vagues grises,
et la pluie commence à tomber,
pour s'éloigner
des falaises effondrées où la terre ocre
et dorée est trop tendre ;
nous sommes en fuite,
cherchant consolation
à l'idée de la catastrophe,
entre les livres vieux, parmi les anciens
meubles qui formaient un intérieur
factice ;
il y avait ce livre d'Aventure et celui
qui racontait la vie qu'on aimerait mener ;
le chocolat, où fondait la crème…
l'heure passait
avec tant de tristesse alentour,
le sens ne se faisait pas,
le tissage,
non,
décidément, du dédale
de l'esprit, du déjà vu,
il fallut sortir.

8 —

Several flowers, printed on the dark background,
can concentrate a past image,
and this perfume that does not belong to them
flows from the drawing;
in this moment, looking at them,
the gray waves close in,
and the rain begins to fall,
to get away
from the crumbled cliffs where the ochre
and golden earth is too tender;
we are in flight,
searching consolation
in the idea of catastrophe,
between old books, among the ancient
furniture that form an artificial
interior;
there was an Adventure book and one
that tells of the life one would like to lead;
chocolate, where cream melted…
the hour passed
with so much surrounding sadness,
the sense was not made,
the weave,
no,
decidedly, some maze
of the spirit, of déjà vu,
one had to go through.

9 —

L'heure de se recueillir :
soleil tombé au sol, feuilles
juxtaposées en taches claires, sombres,
cachent la terre humide où le lent travail se fait,
d'ensevelissement...
faut-il ensevelir l'été ?
Le lac joyeux et phosphorescent ?
Quelques fleurs persistent dans leur couleur
rouges, minuscules, jaunes,
blanches, roses et mauve tendre,
anémiques et belles qui sècheront
cette nuit, peut-être.

9 —

The hour of meditation:
sun fallen to ground, leaves
juxtaposed in clear stains, somber,
hiding the humid earth where the slow work is done
of burial...
must we bury summer?
The happy and phosphorescent lake?
Several flowers persist in their color
red, minuscule, yellow,
white, rose and tender mauve,
anemic and beautiful, drying up
tonight, maybe.

Cet instant unique
se distingue par la pensée qui y naît ;
ces fleurs si rouges, sur un arbuste,
auprès de petites boules blanches...
les travaux agricoles qu'on mène dans
ce champ : ne s'agit-il plus désormais que de
conservation du paysage ?
Les animaux sont là, ils nous regardent,
alors que nous passons :
les veaux, les moutons noirs, si innocents,
tournent leurs yeux vers nous ;
que savons-nous ?
Les châtaignes montrent leur cœur-fruit luisant,
feu du soleil fort, au loin,
qui ranime les bâtiments de brique
d'une lueur hollandaise.
Je marche sur ces routes,
comme du Nord,
un arbre plein d'oiseaux se tait,
à mon approche, des pigeons bleus s'envolent.
La journée s'achève :
les tracteurs rentrent sur les routes,
les employés des villes aussi,
et le soir tombe :
bientôt la nuit, l'abandon.

10 —

This unique instant
distinguishes itself by the thought born there;
these flowers so red, on a shrub,
next to some little white balls...
the farmers one leads to these
fields: from now on is it no longer about
conservation of the countryside?
The animals are here, they watch us,
as we pass:
the calves, the black sheep, so innocent,
turn their eyes toward us;
what do we know?
The chestnuts show their gleaming heart-fruit,
fire of strong sunlight, at a distance,
reanimating the brick buildings
with a Dutch gleam.
I walk these paths,
as from the North,
a tree full of birds hushes
at my approach, blue pigeons take flight.
The day ends:
tractors return by road,
the employees of the city too,
and evening falls:
soon night, release.

Trans. D. Jackson

CHEMINS SE CROISANT

Chaque instant déplie
formes et reflets
sous le réel, voix intérieures,
sensations anciennes,
en ce moment, mêlées :
un tourbillon.
Ne plus être :
l'inacceptable est cela.
Chemins se croisant,
culs-de-sacs, paroles impuissantes ;
comment remonter à la source ?
L'allègement ne vient-il jamais ?
On pourrait crier, à être ainsi
enfermés ;
loin, des chiens se baignant,
des nuages, des papillons ;
tout ce qui est écrit tend à fixer...
et si, autour de cette attache,
les mots pouvaient se faire
arabesques
si cela nous était accordé,
dans le dialogue, l'échange ;

mais tout se fige.

PATHS CROSSING

Each instant unfolds
forms and glints
under the real, interior voices,
old sensations
in this moment, mixed:
a whirlwind.
To be no more:
it is unacceptable.
Paths crossing,
cul-de-sacs, impotent words;
how to climb back to the source?
Will relief never come?
One could shout, to be thus
enclosed;
far off, dogs bathe,
clouds, butterflies;
everything written tends to fix...
and if, around this bond,
the words could make themselves
arabesques
if this was granted us,
in dialogue, the exchange;

but everything freezes.

Trans. D. Jackson

ELSSENEUR

Ce matin fut un commencement.
Et si nous avions dû quitter ce logement,
cette prairie mouillée, passer une dernière fois par
ces sentiers, alors que notre chat noir se roulait encore devant
   nos pas,
comme pour nous empêcher de partir ?
Oui, il s'agissait bien de cela : ne pas partir.
Or, tout se précipitait maintenant et notre vie, déjà, nous ne
   l'avions plus,
le chat même de joyeux qu'il était, aurait ses derniers soubre-
   sauts dans nos bras
et serait enterré là, face à la Méditerranée, sous l'arbre
appelé yucca, enveloppé dans une étoffe précieuse,
tel, maintenant, dans notre souvenir, les chats pharaoniques
appelés à survivre
dans les mémoires et sur les peintures,
gravés, sculptés de pierre noire, lisse et brillante
dans la perfection de leur forme souple ou
emmaillotés, comme le nôtre, avec révérence et amour,
pour toujours, à l'endroit où se trouvent
les deux pommes de pin de la mémoire humaine
et la brassée de mimosa de février.
Il passe encore autour du lit, et
miaule et réclame notre attention, pour toujours.
Ce chat qui nous empêchait de partir,
de quitter le bonheur, maintenant que
nous savions quel il était, quel nom lui donner,
que nous le reconnaissions
et que nous allions encore combattre pour lui et tout faire,
tout ce qui se pouvait, pour reconnaître ce que nous étions :

ELSSINORE

This morning made a beginning.
And what if we had to leave this accommodation,
this wet prairie, pass one last time by
its paths, so that the black cat rolled again before
    our steps
as if to prevent us from leaving?
Yes, it really was about this: to not leave.
However, everything sped up and already our life was ours no
    longer,
the cat, even happy as he was, would have made his last leaps
    into our arms,
and held close there, facing the Mediterranean, under the tree
called yucca, enveloped in a precious fabric,
like, in our memory now, the pharaonic cats,
destined to survive
in memory and paintings,
engraved, sculpted of black stone, smooth and brilliant
in the perfection of their supple form or
swaddled, like ours, with reverence and love
forever, at the place where is found
the two pinecones of human memory
and the sway of the mimosa of February.
It passes again by the bed, and
meows reclaiming our attention, forever.
This cat who prevented our leaving,
to part with happiness, now that
we knew what it was, what name to give it,
that we recognized it
and that we would yet fight for it and do anything,
anything we could, to recognize what we were:

hommes et alliés,
depuis ce moment et pour toujours.
Nous sommes partis.

men and allied,
from this moment and forever.
We left.

Trans. D. Jackson

EN CETTE SAISON

1 —

Les falaises, en cette saison,
peuvent glisser, la boue, les pierres,
être entraînées
et, ce soir
d'orage, il faut renoncer
à renouer avec l'autre voyage
— celui fait il y a des années —,
à le continuer :
impossible de rejoindre, en allant vers le nord,
cette avancée d'autrefois vers le sud.
Le vent fait peur,
l'obscurité est habitée :
en sens inverse, longeant les grèves battues,
on pénètre
le pays ombré des collines,
où s'abriter …
et cette nuit sans sommeil, pourquoi ?
Les vagues, la force d'une idée ?
Enthousiasme malmené,
mené au bord de la solitude,
ordalie ;
l'horizon, frappé de la foudre,
a fondu dans sa propre lumière
et l'air, au-dessus des têtes,
a la subtilité de l'énigme ;
que sacrifier ?
Vers où dérivent les corps endormis
— le don n'est-il pas cela ? —,
abandonnés à l'océan, sans recours, dérivant

IN THIS SEASON

1 —

The cliffs, in this season,
can slip, the mud, the stones,
swept away
and, this evening
of storm, we must give up
connecting to the other voyage
—the one made so many years ago—
to continue it:
impossible to rejoin, going north,
this travel once south.
The wind is scary,
the dark is inhabited:
in the opposite direction, following the beaten shores,
one enters
the shadowed countryside of the hills,
where to take shelter...
and this night without sleep, why?
The waves, the force of an idea?
Mishandled enthusiasm
carried to the edge of solitude,
ordeal;
the horizon, struck by lightning,
melted in its own light
and the air, over head,
has the subtlety of the enigma;
what to sacrifice?
Toward where the sleeping bodies drift
—was this not the gift?—
abandoned to the ocean, without recourse, drifting

jusqu'au matin qui les délie,
où le miroir des flaques et la boue
disent lacune et matière, absence
du geste qui réconcilie ?

until morning releases them,
where the mirror of puddles and mud
say lacuna and material, absence
of the reconciling gesture?

2 —

La nuit prend tout
et les bras, et le souffle le plus délicat,
les moments, enfin, qui ne sont que mémoire,
sombrent dans cet oubli — négation de l'existence.
Ainsi l'Océan Pacifique
et ses rives matinales,
la fenêtre, devant le rivage, et ce regard intranquille
que nous portons sur les choses et les êtres,
cette sérénité, aussi,
(tenant à on ne sait quoi :
un monstre, au loin, satisfait d'une proie,
un équilibre incestueux et momentané entre le manque
et la plénitude)
parmi les invités, aux tables du matin,
entre les couples, les familles se rassasiant.
Quel visage étrange et lumineux que celui
du neuf et du vain,
et cette main tombée et tachée de boue,
il aurait fallu la prendre, qu'elle se recrée
de son ancienne matière,
se recompose
de chair touchable et émouvante.
Tandis que les falaises s'écroulent et que le temps barre
la fuite vers le nord,
les collines de l'intérieur, leurs arrondis encerclent,
offrent de demeurer là,
auprès de la colère. En pensée, les corps reposent toujours
dans les lambeaux des vagues
et les rêves permis dont on ne se réveille pas sans images
vivaces et recueillies :

2 —

The night takes all
and arms, and the most delicate breath,
the moments, at last, which are only memory,
sink into forgetfulness—negation of existence.
Thus the Pacific Ocean
and its morning coasts,
the window, before the coast, and this unsettled look
we cast on things and beings,
this serenity, also,
(holding to who knows what:
a monster, far off, feeds on prey,
an equilibrium incestuous and temporary between need
and plenitude)
among the guests, at the breakfast tables,
between the couples, the families eat their fill.
What a strange and luminous face offer
the new and the vain,
and this hand fallen and stained with mud,
it would have been necessary to take it, that it recreate itself
from its ancient material,
recompose itself
from some touchable and moving flesh.
As long as the cliffs crumble and the weather bars
flight to the north,
the hills of the interior, their curves encircle,
offer to remain there,
beside anger. Thinking, bodies still rest
in the tatters of waves
and the permitted dreams from which one can't wake without
    images
enduring and enrapt:

l'origine du mouvement d'un bras, son suspens,
le visage, les yeux fermés
à la fureur du vent, aux vagues et à l'orage qui ont rendu
   inaccessibles
les routes aperçues ;
quel désordre et quel nouvel ordre cette tempête a créés,
montrant ce qui est juste et rendant implacable
son jugement !

the origin of the movement of an arm, its hanging,
the face, the eyes closed
against the fury of wind, waves and the storm
blocking the perceived paths;
what disorder and what new order this tempest created,
showing what is just and rendering implacable
its judgment!

3 —

Sans élan, mais dans la ferveur,
la voix s'élève,
elle vient après le regard intérieur,
retraversant les distances d'ici
au passé,
des mains pleines
n'osent se dépouiller de leurs ors,
ensevelis naguère ; mais le regard qui
franchit ainsi les strophes du temps
porte cette persistance dans le Désir,
nouveau regard, vrai regard
qui revient de ta traversée souffrante
le plus vrai.
Au fond des minutes de solitude,
ces yeux regardent
sans voile, posés
sur la vérité des distances, la mesure juste
des instants.
Ranime par les mots
les figures du passé,
inscrites dans l'air,
rassemble ces images vives,
puisqu'il n'est
nul mystère, désormais : une sorte de platitude
qui émeut
dans ses variations infinies mais aussi inconnaissables
que le blanc.

3 —

Without force, but with passion,
the voice rises,
it comes after the interior gaze,
recrossing the distances from here
to the past,
full hands
not daring to get rid of their gold,
recently buried; but the gaze that
crosses thus the strophes of time
carries this persistence in Desire,
new gaze, true gaze
that returns from your suffering epoch
most true.
In the heart of these minutes of solitude,
the eyes gaze
without veil, posed
on the truth of distances, the just measure
of instants.
Revive with words
figures of the past,
inscribed in the air,
reassemble these living images,
for there is
no longer any mystery, from now on: a sort of platitude
that moves
in its infinite variations but as unknowable
as blank.

4 —

Comment le froid entre-t-il
dans les veines ?
Comment faire
cesser ce frisson ?
La baie au loin, la ville et ces ponts qui relient
et séparent,
en montant la pente de la colline
bâtie de maisons de bois,
pas d'apaisement,
cette parole
de la veille au soir
avait fait son chemin dans le corps ;
impossible, ce dialogue,
rien n'allait
et peut-être rien n'irait ;
acidité des heures :

— N'est-ce pas la même chose ?
N'y a-il pas qu'une seule chose ?

4 —

How does cold enter
the veins?
How to
stop shivering?
The bay at a distance, the city and its bridges that join
and separate,
climbing the slope of the hill
built with wooden houses,
no appeasement,
this word
from yesterday evening
had made its path in the body;
impossible, this dialogue,
nothing went well
and maybe nothing will;
acidity of hours:

—Isn't it the same thing?
Isn't it that there's only one thing?

Trans. D. Jackson

LE DAUPHIN

Derrière la vitre, à une table, une silhouette tout engoncée,
manteau noir, bonnet de laine ;
sur le bord de la fenêtre : des cruches à eau de verre,
mais nulle menthe épanouie,
au delà du bar, une étagère avec du thé Lipton
rouge et jaune, un sac de sucre.

Un plastique transparent vole sur la chaussée,
entre les bus qui se croisent,
une femme a la main dans la bouche,
d'autres voyageurs, agrippés aux lanières ou assis, certains
    déploient un journal.
Voici le square,
lumineux à cette heure où toutes les couleurs s'atténuent,
plus d'ombre sous les arbres, mais la clarté
réverbérée d'un mur d'immeuble, très blanc.
Dans le boyau sinueux,
déséquilibré, innervé de Metallica,
s'avance Haine,
voué au bracelet de force à pointes,
aux dreadlocks et lanières, d'un héroïsme de ce temps ;
la travée est muette.
On est transporté derrière la cage fumée du bus,
habillée des affiches de "l'École paternelle"
d'Eddie Murphy,
reflets sur les vitres de visages
traversés
d'ombres qui se déforment et fuient, captées par la surface
    brillante ;
sur la ligne, avant de tourner, on passe
devant "Chez Ebru", snack turc,

LE DAUPHIN

Behind the pane, at a table, a cramped silhouette,
black overcoat, knit cap;
at the edge of the window: a glass water pitcher,
but no blooming mint,
behind the bar, a shelf with Lipton Tea
red and yellow, a bag of sugar.

A clear plastic sack flies on the median strip,
between passing buses,
a woman has her hand in her mouth,
some travelers hanging from the straps, others unfold
    newspapers.
Look at the square
luminous at this hour when every color softens,
no more shadows under the trees, but the light
reflects from the white of an apartment wall.
In the twisted gut,
reeling, strung out on Metallica,
comes Hate,
devotee of the studded cuff,
dreadlocks and straps, a heroism for these latter days;
the row is quiet.
We're carried behind the tinted cage of the bus,
dressed in posters for Eddie Murphy's
"Daddy Day Care"
reflections on the glass of faces
crossed
with shadows that disintegrate and disappear, caught on the
    brilliant surface;
on the bus route, before turning, we pass
in front of "Ebru's," Turkish take-out,

où une file attend pour un sandwich ;
à l'angle,
les immenses baies du deuxième sont éclairées comme pour
    une fête,
non, l'orange des lampadaires enflamme les vitres.
Le Dauphin, avant l'aube,
est un repaire d'hommes seuls ;
venus se chauffer, ils tiennent entre leurs mains leur tasse,
le grill à pizzas est encore éteint
et les néons ont dépecé la pièce nue par leur blancheur ;
ce sont les mots rose électrique : self, sandwich, qui attirent ici,
et le chemin quotidien.

Certains matins, c'est le marché sous la rampe du métro ;
entre les étalages et les camions, des maraîchers déchargent
alors qu'il fait encore nuit, on mange des soupes au Dauphin,
des travailleurs ont mis entre eux un sac jaune
avec des choses à partager.
Plus tard, la foule des hommes
investissent mondial-phone-internet,
vont fumer devant chez Goutex et dans le renfoncement de
    la poste
où des enfants noirs
crient et courent après un ballon.
Ils sont là, appuyés aux murs.
Devant la crèche et son cortège d'animaux inoffensifs
dessinés en des paysages pacifiés,

where a line is waiting for a sandwich;
on the corner,
the immense bay windows on the third floor are lit as if for a
    party,
no, the orange of the streetlamps is dousing the window panes
    in flame.
Le Dauphin, before dawn,
is a haunt for lonely men;
having come to warm themselves up, they hold their cups in
    their hands,
the pizza grill is still off
and the neon lights have dismembered the naked room with
    their whiteness;
these are the words, electric pink: self, sandwich, that lure,
the daily round.

Some mornings, it's the market beneath the rails of the elevated;
between the stalls and trucks, the farmers unpack
while it's still night, they eat soup at Le Dauphin,
some workers brought a yellow bag
with something to share.
Later, the crowd of men
mobbing global–phone–internet,
will smoke in front of Goutex's and in the ditch in front of the
    post office
where black kids
yell and run after a ball.
They're there, resting against the wall.
In front of the nursery school and its menagerie of
    non-threatening animals
drawn in pacified landscapes,

les désœuvrés, par groupes de deux ou trois,
s'adossent aux platanes minces encagés,
se juchent sur les barrières, ils occupent la rue, proposent
Marlboro, portables…
L'écrivain public
attend au carrefour,
les coiffeurs sur le seuil de leur salon ;
et, venus du boulevard, les passants qui se hâtent,
les femmes, les enfants, arrivent là,
et leur élan se perd à ce croisement,
enclave de l'activité diurne illicite, où s'échangent
les produits du petit larcin et des trafics,
les combines, et l'Ennui.

loiterers, in groups of two or three,
lean against caged and slender plane trees,
perched on the barriers, they occupy the road, offering
Marlboros, cell phones…
The public writer
waits at the crossroads,
the hairdressers on the threshold of their salons;
and, having come from the boulevard, the rushing pedestrians,
women, children, get here,
and their bodies give out at this crossing,
enclave of illicit activity in broad daylight, where they trade
the fruits of petty larceny and trafficking,
schemes, and Boredom.

Trans. J.B. Anderson

ÉNIGME

Dessins nés de la peinture écaillée,
pourquoi vous faire parler ?
Énigme
d'usure et de résistance,
apparition flamboyante qu'on aimerait d'un sens,
ajout, commentaire
et retour à la fin,
manuscrit où lire l'envers des choses…

Que ces lettres
soient châteaux,
surgis d'encre et de boue,
dessinés !
Que le dialogue
renaisse et flambe,
consumant l'air des mots,
apaisant les souffles hâtifs,
découvrant les rêves sépia comme paysages
traversés où retourner !
Il y a les livres et il y a ce métal
usé, cette autre matière de l'écriture,
aléatoire, dont on use comme d'un miroir
de l'esprit, et qui résiste
à qui cherche.

ENIGMA

Drawings born of scaly painting,
why force you to speak?
Enigma
of attrition and resistance,
flamboyant apparition that one liked to have of a meaning
addition, commentary
and returning to the end
manuscript where one reads the reverse side of things…

May these letters
be castles,
risen from ink and mud,
designed!
May dialogue
be reborn and burn,
consuming the air of words,
appeasing hurried breaths,
discovering sepia dreams like countrysides
to return to!
There are books and there is this worn
metal, this other material of writing,
aleatory, that one uses like a mirror
of the spirit, that resists
the one searching.

Trans. D. Jackson

LA TOUR LUMIÈRE

D'après *Nun,* d'Helmut Lachenmann
et avec quelques phrases de Nicolas Schöffer
— à propos de sa *Tour Lumière Cybernétique*

THE LIGHT TOWER

From *Nun*, by Helmut Lachenmann
and with some lines by Nicolas Schöffer
— about his *Cybernetic Light Tower*

LA TOUR

... je suis arrivé à un point de rupture totale avec le
passé. J'ai alors créé le spatiodynamisme, c'est-à-dire
l'utilisation de l'espace en tant que matériau de base
exclusif de mes structures. Par la suite, j'ai ajouté à
l'espace la lumière et surtout le temps. Ainsi, je suis
devenu programmateur de ces trois matériaux ...

Remuement intense, bleu,
centrifugeuses, mais aussi océan,
cris, une poulie monte un décor,
aussitôt vaporisé ;
ces envols ! frôlements aériens,
point d'orgue,
on entre :
est-ce une jungle ?
un sous-bois ?
et l'on s'avance encore, bonds et frottements, bruissement
du monde, ravissement et réveil incessant des désirs.

Que penses-tu
devant la goutte d'eau
projetée sur l'écran ?
S'y joue la mêlée sans fin
d'un animal aquatique dévorant
un autre qui ne l'a pas encore
avalé, déjà englouti
à demi par le premier,
corps translucides,
pinces et pattes arrachées, entrailles sucées, aspirées,
tête sectionnée ; il n'a plus sa queue,
qu'il mange encore, qu'il arrache

THE TOWER

... I arrived at a point of total rupture with the past.
So I created spatiodynamism, which is to say the
utilization of space in such a way as to make it the
exclusive base material of my structures. Then, I added
to space light and finally, time. Thus, I became
programmer of these three materials...

Intense moving, blue,
centrifugal, but also ocean,
shouts, a pulley raises a setting,
soon vaporized;
what flights! aerial frolicking,
organ fermata,
one enters:
is it a jungle?
an undergrowth?
and one advances further, leaps and frictions, rustlings
of the world, rapture and incessant waking of desires.

What do you think
before the drop of water
cast on the screen?
There plays the endless melee
of an aquatic animal devouring
another that it hasn't yet
gulped down, just half-
swallowed,
translucent bodies,
claws and feet torn, entrails sucked, inhaled,
head sectioned; the tail it has no more,
that it eats still, that it tears

de son bec cartilagineux
la chair de l'autre.
Poursuite, dans cette flaque, de combattants minuscules,
pour survivre…
instants brefs, extensibles qui se muent en fanfares discordantes :
l'humanité face au désordre s'amplifiant,
son avancée vers la connaissance
d'alentour et de soi, dans ce monde ensauvagé
avec ses pressentiments et ses découvertes…

Des pas dans l'ombre, la nuit se fait
dans la pensée, malgré ta résistance, ton effort pour parler,
lentement tu te rends à la fascination
d'une écoute sans brouillage.
C'est le premier son du matin ou le chant
de la première étoile,
la pluie fine mouille à peine, mais sonne ;
une aile dégage la perspective qui, d'acier sur azur,
crisse et se dénude.

> En effet, ma tour n'est pas un objet. Son armature,
> conçue aussi légère que possible, n'est qu'un
> échafaudage destiné à supporter une idée. L'idée, c'est
> le rôle primordial de la cybernétique en art. Dans des
> sociétés devenues massives et mouvantes comme les
> nôtres, on ne peut plus en effet concevoir l'art sous
> forme d'objets individuels qu'on commercialise et sur
> lesquels on spécule. L'art pour tous doit remplacer l'art
> pour les privilégiés. Or, précisément, les concepts,
> aléatoires, permettent des combinaisons à l'infini, qui
> peuvent s'adapter à un environnement social fluide, le
> refléter, et répercuter pour chacun les caractéristiques
> de l'ensemble.

with its cartilaginous beak
the flesh of the other.
Then, in this pool, the chase of tiny fighters,
to survive...
brief, extendable instants that morph in discordant fanfare:
humanity faced with growing chaos,
its progress toward awareness
of surroundings and self, in this world made wild
by premonitions and discoveries...

Some footsteps into shadow, night makes itself
in thought, despite your resistance, your effort to speak,
slowly you surrender to the fascination
of a listening without static.
It's the first sound of the morning or the song
of the first star,
the mist moistens barely, but rings out;
a wing clears the perspective of steel on azure that
squeaks and bares itself.

> *Indeed, my tower isn't an object. Its framework,
> conceived as lightly as possible, is no more than
> scaffolding destined to support an idea. The idea
> here is the primordial role of the cybernetic in art.
> In societies as massive and mobile as ours, one can
> no longer effectually conceive art under the form
> of individual objects that can be commercialized
> and on which one speculates. Art for all must
> replace art for the privileged ones. Now, more
> precisely, the concepts, the aleatory ones, permit
> infinite combinations that can fit to a fluid social
> environment, reflect it, and echo for each person
> the characteristics of the group.*

Surprise devant l'inconnu, il y a, au loin,
des trains qui partent — panorama découvert —
et soudain l'éclair, la netteté du mal :
jugement et poids
des choses, appréciation de leur déplacement.

Reprise de l'élan :
les images, les significations s'enchaînent
…
tu entres dans l'effroyable.
On va sous les coupoles
et les corps dansent, se souvenant des tortures, toujours :
tu entends, dans les chambres, les cris, distinctement,
et des sifflements,

voici la longue file de ceux
qu'on emmène.

Surprise before the unknown, far off,
trains leaving—panorama discovered—
and suddenly lightning, the clarity of evil:
judgment and weight
of things, appreciation for their displacement.

New impetus:
images, the significations follow
…
you enter the horror.
We're going under the domes
and the bodies dance, remembering tortures, still:
you hear distinctly, in the rooms, shouts
and squeals,

here's the long line of those
we lead away.

Trans. D. Jackson

CELLULE

Seul, dans sa cellule ou la cabine du bateau,
un homme est debout, dans son propre cerveau :
ces sons entendus, ces craintes
résonnent, pour lui, autrement.

Dans le lointain, les cloches d'une église, mais isolée,
qui n'est plus un appel,
mais le chant de mort de l'oiseau,
entendu, cette fois, clairement

et la voix de cette femme,
prise, elle, dans un opéra, d'où naissent espoir et danger :

un feu gagne,
voici les ombres des disparus qui, dans ce vacarme,
avancent, timides,
nommés par leurs propres noms, ils ont leurs gestes habituels
    et connus,
le temps est compté pour parler ;

quelques mots seront échangés
entre cette femme et cet homme,
tandis qu'ils avancent, d'un même pas, dans le clair-obscur.

Le présent qui permet, sous les arceaux d'accords, l'émoi,
— accords répétés et crissement des grillons
qui font revenir les étés, avec les ivresses —
le chant de la mer et des embarcadères, le sillon des paquebots,
nous l'avons vu se creuser, ouvrir
cette vie sur le néant,

CELL

In his cell or the cabin of the boat
alone, a man stands in his head:
the sounds heard, the fears
resonate differently for him.

In the distance, the bells of a church, but isolated
which is no longer a call,
but the death song of a bird,
heard clearly this time

and the voice of that woman
taken from an opera where hope and danger are born:

a fire spreads,
here are the shadows of the disappeared who, in this racket
advance, timid,
named by their own names, they have their habitual and
    recognized gestures
the time to talk is numbered;

several words will be exchanged
between that woman and that man
while they advance, keeping pace, through the half-light.

The present that permits, under harmonious arches, turmoil,
—agreements repeated to the grating of crickets
that make summer return, drunkenly—
the song of the sea and the piers, the furrows of liners,
we saw it widen, open
life to nothing,

malgré les paroles que nous échangions ;
il y avait cette déchirure dans la nuit,
et de la lumière sur le revers de la vague.

Le paquebot s'est figé dans un musée,
non loin des formes portuaires sans plan incliné,
la rouille méditative travaille les cônes enchâssés
que l'on contourne par des couloirs s'étrécissant : le centre,
plaque de béton délimitée par l'ombre, s'étend,
nous prend...

qu'y a-t-il que tu ne peux nommer
sur cette rive au jardin délaissé,

tu t'enivres à ce chant et fixes du regard l'écueil,
gardes en toi la tempête.

Où est le port, désormais : ses allées sableuses, ses bars
et ses constructions basses où tu revenais : grues,
remorqueurs, soleil couchants de cartes postales ?

despite the words we shared;
there was a wrenching in the night,
and light on the wrong side of the wave.

The liner is frozen in a museum,
not far from the port-like docks without inclined plane,
the meditative rust works the inserted cones
that one goes around by narrowing halls: the center,
concrete plaque defined by shadow, stretching,
taking us...

what is it there that you cannot name
on the shore of this neglected garden,

exhilarating in the song you fix your gaze on the reef,
keeping in you the storm.

Where is the port, now: its sandy paths, its bars
and low structures where you would return: cranes,
tugs, postcard sunsets?

Trans. D. Jackson

VILLE

... une ville, depuis le matin jusqu'au soir, et encore du soir jusqu'à l'aube, cela vit, cela grouille, cela traverse une série d'activités, avec des baisses ou des hausses continues de tension. Les gens marchent, prennent le métro, le train, leur voiture, consomment du gaz, de l'électricité, regardent la télévision, travaillent, mangent, s'équipent, circulent. Il pleut, il y a du soleil. La Bourse monte, descend. Les agences de presse font crépiter les téléscripteurs. Et tout ce potentiel quotidien d'énergies, qui constitue la fièvre variable de la cité, n'avait jusqu'ici été capté par aucun instrument.

Délié de tout,
de la vie de naguère, des mots mêmes,

— Les muer en chant,
tenter encore...

dans cette accélération,
il doit vivre le cri
que porte l'air ;
annonces, départs :
il avait en lui le frémissement du jour
...
qui ne le retient plus.

Suivre le vol qui se détache,
tu te détaches,
mots sans lien,
passent, ombres sur ta vie,
tumulte des foules, sifflements des gares,
s'éloignent.

CITY

...a city, from morning till evening, and again from evening until dawn, lives, teems, it encompasses a series of activities, with low or high spectra of voltage. People walk, take the metro, the train, their car, consuming gas, electricity, watching television, working, eating, outfitting themselves, circulating. It rains, there's sun. The stock market climbs, drops. The press makes teleprinters crackle. And all this quotidian potential of energies, which constitutes the variable fever of the city, had not until now been captured by any instrument.

Untied from everything,
from the life of not long ago, from words even,

—To change them in song,
trying still...

in this acceleration,
he must live the shout
ringing in the air;
announcements, departures:
he had in him the shiver of day
...
that no longer holds him back.

To follow the flight that breaks free,
you free yourself,
words without ties,
pass, shadows on your life,
uproar of crowds, whistles of train stations,
growing distant.

La pluie tombe maintenant sur l'Hudson,
des rafales noires, moins de clarté,
ramages agités à la surface,
ruissellements sur les vitres du train ;
un homme en costume travaille sur ses genoux,
qu'écrit-il ? il ne jette pas un regard au paysage
détrempé d'encre de Chine,
aux pointillés qui barrent l'image mouvante...

Cependant tu t'étais endormie, les traits tombaient sur le
    fleuve.
Les barques de pêcheurs
— ce n'était pas une eau-forte, mais les autres hommes,
derrière la vitre —,
et le train filait ;

mais nous pouvions poursuivre,
dans le grondement du fleuve et du Temps ;
les poteaux électriques, noircis, se jettent
contre les wagons, s'abolissent, eux aussi déformés.

Ce moment d'orage et de repos,
et puis, l'absence de lutte,
l'abandon à la course du train
qui entre dans la ville,
longe les hauts immeubles de brique
aux vitres brisées ; les impasses barbelées
heurtent les rails, et les carrés
de terrain vague exposent leurs carcasses,
matelas, bidons amoncelés ;
devant une façade aux fenêtres béantes
et noircies, dans un renfoncement,
une bande hurle et rit :
des enfants descendus de la cité
font cercle autour de deux télés,

The rain falls now on the Hudson,
black gusts, less light,
agitated leaf patterns on the surface,
streaming on the windows of the train;
a man in a suit works on his knees,
what's he writing? He doesn't glance at the countryside
drenched in India ink,
at the dots striking out the moving image...

While you were asleep, the lines fell into the river.
The fishing boats
—it wasn't an etching but other men,
behind the window—,
and the train rushed off;

but we could follow,
in the rumble of the river and the Weather;
the power poles, darkened, throw themselves
against the coaches, toss themselves out, they're out of shape
    too.

This moment of storm and of rest,
and then the absence of struggle,
abandoning will to the course of the train
entering the city,
along the tall brick buildings
with broken windows; the alleys blocked with barbed wire
at the rails, and the squares
of waste ground exposing their carcasses,
mattresses, piled drums;
before a facade of windows opened
and darkened, in a recess,
a crowd yells and laughs:
children descended from the projects
form a circle around two TVs,

ersatz de grand écran, et d'autres les rejoignent,
pour voir...

Et cette prairie d'autrefois...
on voit des rails, au bout, les trains
passent par instants
et au-dessus, le ciel est intensément,
mais doucement étendu, moiré de floraisons
neigeuses qui se forment là, et se distendent,
trace et souvenir du printemps,
de son éveil.

La couverture de ton livre rappelle d'autres prairies en pente.
Cheltenham from Leckhampton Hill ;

que font maintenant ces personnages : la femme
à la robe rouge et au chapeau, qui dessinait,
et l'homme qui, de son bras tendu, lui montrait
un point du paysage ?

On peut sauter dans des ronds et des carrés,
se laisser enfermer dans la prison de lumière,
aux barres rougies au feu, ou blanches, incandescentes
et soumettre son corps au tressautement d'images filmées,
passer derrière un buisson de métal bruissant,
façonné à la lampe à souder,
et qui ne porte pas de fruits,
se jeter sous une épave de voiture,
calcinée, abandonnée
par ses occupants
— où sont-ils ? —,
se reposer sur un banc au bord d'une sente de gravier,
en écoutant les oiseaux dont le chant enregistré
est diffusé par haut-parleur.

fake big screen, and others join them,
to see...

And this prairie of another time...
one sees the rails, at the end, trains
pass at moments
and above, the sky is intensely,
but gently stretched out, watered by snowy
blooms that form there, and stretch,
trace and memory of Spring,
of its waking.

Your book's jacket recalls other sloping prairies.
Cheltenham from Leckhampton Hill;

what are these characters doing now: the woman
in the red dress and hat, drawing,
and the man who, pointing, showed her
a spot of countryside?

One could leap into the circles and squares,
let oneself be enclosed in the prison of light,
with bars heated red hot, or white, incandescent,
to submit body to the twitching of filmed images,
to pass behind a shrub of rustling metal,
fashioned by the lamp to merge,
and bearing no fruit,
to throw oneself under a wrecked car,
charred, abandoned
by its occupants
—where are they?—
to rest on a bank at the edge of a gravel path,
listening to the birds whose recorded song
is diffused by loudspeaker.

Ça ne fait pas mal, ce n'est qu'une répétition
du jour de l'ultime souffrance…

à chaque pas regardant en arrière
et loin en avant, nos yeux cherchent,
parmi cette confusion des êtres et des choses,
perçoivent un renouveau,
…
et parfois, nous découvrons là, tout près,
une nature, envols et sifflements, une respiration
en vagues, de sons jumeaux ou contrariés.

> … *ma tour sera le tensiomètre, le baromètre, le ther-*
> *momètre, l'oscillomètre, l'enregistreur permanent du*
> *pouls de la ville. Grâce à des circuits de téléscripteurs*
> *et d'ordinateurs, nous recevrons jour et nuit dans le*
> *socle de la tour et sur les six plates-formes toutes les*
> *données utiles, celles qui concernent le mouvement*
> *des corps (solides, liquides, gazeux), et celles qui*
> *relèvent de l'information. Nous pourrons capter des*
> *signaux venant des administrations locales (comme la*
> *Préfecture, les P et T, la SNCF, la RATP, l'AFP, l'Aéro-*
> *port de Paris, l'Office météorologique, la Bourse,*
> *l'Observatoire, etc.), mais aussi des administrations*
> *régionales, nationales, voire de l'Europe entière. Grâce*
> *à cette sorte de contrôle permanent des fonctions, nous*
> *déterminerons à chaque moment le degré absolu*
> *d'excitation (une sorte de résultante) soit à Paris,*
> *soit en France, soit en Europe.*

It does not hurt, is no more than a repetition
of the day of ultimate suffering...

at each step looking behind
and far in advance, our eyes search,
among this confusion of beings and things,
perceive a renewal,
...
and sometimes, we discover here, very close,
a countryside, flights and whistles, breathing
in waves, of sounds joined or contrary.

> *...my tower will be the tensiometer, the barometer, the thermometer, the oscillometer, the permanent recorder of the pulse of the city. Thanks to the circuits of the teleprinters and computers, we will receive day and night at the base of the tower and the six platforms all the useful information, that which concerns the movement of bodies (solids, liquids, gases), and those dependent on the information. We could capture the signals coming from the local administrations (like the Prefecture, the P and T, the SNCF, the RATP, the AFP, the Airport of Paris, the Meteorology Office, the stock market, the Observatory, etc.), but also the regional, national administrations, or even those of the rest of Europe. Thanks to this kind of permanent monitoring of functions, we will determine at each moment the absolute degree of excitation (a sort of resultant) whether in Paris, France, or Europe.*

Trans. D. Jackson

ÉVEIL

Éveil, le premier jour,
les pales du ventilateur ;
ces ondes créent l'espace
à travers le store à lamelles,
des pignons hollandais de briques
adoucies par le soleil, vibrations.

Ce sursaut,
avant l'aube, des camions, en bas,
enfance de la perception et variété ;
puis, des appels viennent ensemble, moteur, porte,
chien,
frôlement : le tactile dans le son,
expérience et découverte,
à l'origine de la parole ;
le Vent se lève :

appareillage du jour,
tangage
...
son esprit
est indécis ; puis sa perception s'affine :
dessin de hauts bâtiments,
délimitation de quartiers, tous reliés,
énumération des travaux des hommes,
qui commencent, s'achèvent,
appels entendus, écho,
curiosité,
chaleur et pluie, leur parfum,
souvenir des variations du jour,

AWAKENING

Awakening, the first day,
the blades of the fan;
its waves create space
across the strips of the blinds,
the Dutch gable of bricks
softened by sun, vibrations.

This jolt,
before sunrise, of trucks below,
childhood of perception and variety;
then, calls come together, motor, door,
dog,
rustling: the tactile in sound,
experience and discovery,
at the origin of language;
the Wind rises:

casting off for the day,
rolling
...
its spirit
is unsure; then its perception narrows:
design of tall buildings,
boundary of neighborhoods, all linked,
enumeration of the works of men,
that begins, concludes,
heard calls, echo,
curiosity,
heat and rain, their perfume,
memory of the variations of day,

soirée où le soleil descend,
spectacle dans les villes,
théâtres, cinémas, cafés, foule dérivant sur les trottoirs,

le reflet de l'esprit, dans le miroir de Venise ;
un vieil homme vient de l'arrière-boutique :
que veut-il ?
Il vient dire, doucement souriant,
la vertu des objets qu'il a disposés ici,
les encriers de porcelaine chinoise

et le tableau d'une pêche nocturne,
éclairée par la lune,
huile sur bois ;
elle sort d'un nuage,
disque blanc sur fond outremer,
un phare se reflète dans l'eau
et des silhouettes de pêcheurs se détachent,
sur le quai, parmi les masses
figurant les ballots ;
l'homme au filet étend les bras,
s'y débat, celui à la canne
s'est avancé vers le large, sur un rocher ;
à gauche, une caravelle va
vers le fond, où la matière s'allège
et brille, fait vivre la nuit ;

il y descend,

mémoire, qui retient les rues
où il s'est promené en rêve.
Il sait qu'il les a vues,

evening when the sun descends,
spectacle in the cities,
theatres, cinemas, cafés, crowd drifting on sidewalks,

the reflection of the spirit, in the mirror of Venice;
an old man comes from the back shop:
what does he want?
He comes to tell, softly smiling,
the virtue of the objects he displayed here,
the ink wells of Chinese porcelain

and the picture of night fishing,
lit by the moon,
oil on wood;
it exits from a cloud,
white disc on ultramarine background,
a lighthouse reflected in water
and the silhouettes of fishers stand out,
on the quay, among the masses
representing bundles;
the man with the net stretches out his arm,
struggles within, the one with the cane
advanced toward the open sea, on a rock;
to the left, a caravel goes
toward the background, where matter lightens
and shines, makes the night live;

he descends here,

memory, holding the streets
where he promenades in dream.
He knows that he saw them,

mais ne s'en souvient plus comme réelles,
il ne se les rappelle que rêvées,
maintes fois rêvées.

but no longer remembers them as real,
he remembers them only as dreams,
many times dreamed.

Trans. D. Jackson

RÊVÉE

La découverte
n'est pas accomplie,
plans raturés d'architectes
sur calques bleutés,
ébauches d'une cité, loin d'ici,
dans un panorama de forêts neuves et préhistoriques,
devant une mer intacte — qui n'existent pas.

Les conversations,
les concerts vertigineux, les représentations fastueuses,
se donnent dans une disharmonie totale :
les exclamations, les appels
des hommes et des animaux qui viennent
à notre rencontre, se mêlent ainsi ;

le petit singe fait des gestes hiératiques,
au fond d'un coton imprimé, il a
des fruits énormes qui se fendent au soleil...

parmi les sphères,
tu avances :

des portes s'ouvrent,
tu parles — on te répond,

premiers fils du canevas.

DREAMED

The discovery
isn't complete,
crossed out plans of architects
on bluish tracing paper,
rough shapes of a city, far from here,
in a panorama of forests new and prehistoric,
before an intact sea—that do not exist.

The conversations,
vertiginous concerts, sumptuous representations,
perform in complete disharmony:
the exclamations, calls
of men and animals who come
to our meeting, mingling thus;

the small ape makes hieratic gestures,
in the depths of printed cotton, he has
some enormous fruits that split in the sun...

among the spheres
you advance:

some doors open,
you speak—someone answers you,

first threads of the canvas.

Trans. D. Jackson

VEILLES...

À Allan Evans

... en fourreaux de peau,
cuir, latex, vinyl,
d'une animalité d'emprunt,
elles sortent à trois d'un taxi,
fendent le cercle des hommes
qui fument sur le trottoir,
devant les buildings,
le cuivre, la vitre des portes à tambour, flashent...

« I am the boss, follow me ».

Quel rôle joue-t-il ?
il nous dira bientôt son nom :
Frankie Machine, Valentine Xavier, ou Travis Bickle...
qu'il incarne dans la rue.

Les images du monde entier
sortent de l'ombre, leur point
d'attache est cette bibliothèque,
collection des écrits et des sons ;
son projet :
rendre aux hommes leur tradition,
vivante,
modèle auquel s'affronter dans une lutte
joyeuse et sans fin.

Manhattan, là-bas, dans le lointain gris,
sa maison est encombrée de figurines,
d'instruments.

SLEEPLESS NIGHTS...

To Allan Evans

...in wrappings of skin,
leather, latex, vinyl,
with a borrowed animalism,
three women exit a taxi,
push through the circle of men
who smoke on the walk,
before the buildings,
the copper, the window of the revolving doors, flash...

"I am the boss, follow me."

What role does he play?
Soon he will tell us his name:
Frankie Machine, Valentine Xavier, or Travis Bickle...
whom he plays in the street.

Images of the entire world
exit the shadow, their point
of attachment is this library,
collection of writings and sounds;
his project:
to give back to men their own tradition,
living,
model that he will brave in a fight
joyous and without end.

Manhattan, over there, in distant gray,
his house is cluttered with figurines,
instruments.

Avant même de commencer à parler,
il prend sa guitare et nous joue
trois blues appris du Rev. Gary Davis
— l'arbitre des élégances—,
il apporte des CDs, les joue, trente secondes,
une minute,
c'est un enregistrement rare d'une pianiste
française, d'agrégats sonores de Java,

le soleil par les vitraux, sur la table,
les tasses, les bras, les visages,
rouge, jaune et vert,
flamme voyageuse…

les Balinais m'ont dit :
on ne peut plus jouer ainsi,
virtuoses avec aisance.

Supposez que la Bourse s'excite, certains violets peuvent
dominer. En cas de grève des chemins de fer, le rouge
s'éteint, remplacé par le bleu. Embouteillages sur les
sorties d'autoroutes, le rouge s'amplifie, et la vitesse se
fixe, tout redevient bleu. Naturellement, nous passerons
des conventions avec le public, de même que sur les
plages, par mer forte, on hisse le drapeau rouge, et tout
le monde comprend la signification. Nous utiliserons
également plus de deux mille flashes électroniques, et les
rayons de vingt-cinq lasers. Au sommet de la tour, des
projecteurs puissants lanceront des faisceaux jusqu'à
deux kilomètres de hauteur. L'allumage et l'extinction
de ces projecteurs, lasers et flashes, dépendront du
cerveau central.

Before even beginning to talk,
he takes his guitar and plays us
three blues learned from Rev. Gary Davis
—arbiter of elegance—
he brings CDs, plays them, thirty seconds,
a minute,
it's a rare recording of a French
pianist, sonorous aggregates of Java,

the sunlight in the stained glass, on the table,
the glasses, the arms, the faces,
red, yellow and green,
traveling flame...

the Balinese told me:
one can't play like this anymore,
virtuosos with ease.

> *Suppose that the stock market becomes excited, certain*
> *violets could stand out. In case of a railroad strike, the*
> *red put out, replaced by blue. Traffic jams at the highway*
> *exits, the red increases, and the quickness established, all*
> *becomes blue again. Naturally, we will conclude agree-*
> *ments with the public, of the same kind as on beaches,*
> *for a strong sea, one hoists the red flag, and everybody*
> *understands the signification. We will equally use more*
> *than two thousand electric flashes, and the rays of*
> *twenty-five lasers. At the summit of the tower, powerful*
> *projectors will cast beams up to two kilometers high.*
> *The lighting and the unlighting of the projectors, lasers*
> *and flashes, will depend on the central brain.*

> *Trans. D. Jackson*

NAUFRAGÉS

On avance au bord
du dicible, c'est là,
dans cette mise en scène grandiose,
que l'homme peut parler ;
inquiet — sans repos.

Les hélicoptères décollent,
leur ventre brillant
s'élève au-dessus du pont du bateau :
ils survolent la baie, la surveillent,
atterrissent sur la plate-forme proche ;

en bas de l'échelle de fer,
une fois accoutumé au noir,
(instruments de mesure, cordages, machines,
rouillés, oxydés, rongés, cassés)
on ne peut ignorer, scintillant dans cette nuit,
plus que nuit, cette nuit troublée
de mort,
les paillettes diamantines, prises
dans les interstices,
traces de fêtes englouties
dans la non-mémoire
de la cale,
nous, naufragés d'ici,
sur les échafaudages de fer élevés,
passons aussi, à toute vitesse, et sans mémoire, dans ces
      trains,
à hauteur des affiches panoramiques
ou des lettres géantes boulonnées sur quadrillé métallique ;
les bolides nickelés se cabrent sur le ciel,

CASTAWAYS

We press toward the edge
of the speakable, there
in this grandiose production
man can speak,
worried—without resting.

Helicopters take off,
their shining belly
rises above the boat's bridge:
they fly over the bay, survey it,
land on the near platform;

at the bottom of the steel ladder,
once accustomed to the dark,
(measuring instruments, riggings, machines,
rusted, oxidized, eroded, shattered)
we can't ignore, glimmering in this night,
more than night, this night troubled
by death,
the diamantine specks caught
in the interstices,
traces of gulped-down feasts
in the non-memory
of the hold,
we castaways from here
on the raised scaffoldings of steel,
we pass by also, at due speed, and without memory, in these
    trains,
to the height of panoramic posters
or giant letters bolted on metallic squares;
the nickel-plated meteors rise to the sky,

tandis que le long du trottoir, des vitrines,
des stores, des murs,
nos ombres difformes passent,
fuient,
et, dans les flaques, s'ouvrent
des puits d'architectures
qui font du sol la surface d'un vertige.

Les sens s'éveillent ;
bruits de départs
et pensées neuves,
les objets reparaissent
déformés,
comme nos visages en plastiline,
par le grotesque des situations.
Nous habitons une nouvelle solitude,
en compagnie du chien,
du son-oiseau, gouttes de pluie
…
— Envols merveilleux…
— De quels oiseaux ?

…
— Que répondent les hommes aux oiseaux ?
— Ces grincements de rouages, clous qu'on rive, fouets,
sifflets de départs,
bruits ou bruitages,
oiseaux mécaniques, oiseaux enregistrés…
— Quelle réponse font les vrais oiseaux aux hommes ?
— Ils les font frémir d'émotion.

so that along the sidewalk, shop windows,
stores, walls,
our deformed shadows pass by,
flee,
and in the puddles, open
architectural wells,
which make of the soil a dizzying surface.

The senses awaken:
noises of departures
and new thoughts,
objects reappear
deformed,
like our faces in plastiline,
by the grotesque in these situations.
We inhabit a new solitude,
in the company of the dog,
of sound-bird, drops of rain.
...
"—Marvelous flights!
—What kind of birds?

...
—How are men responding to the birds?
—The creaking of the gears, bolts that are fastened, lashes,
departure whistles,
noises or sound effects,
mechanical birds, recorded birds...
—What answer will the real birds offer men?
—They make them tremble with emotion."

Trans. M. Kallet

UNE AUTRE VILLE

Tu es seul
dans la ville
avec cette menace
que l'oiseau, d'entre tes mains,
ne s'envole,
et ne te laisse muet,
sachant seulement suivre des yeux
son essor.

L'inquiétude est encore
derrière le jour qui se lève…
ô cette clarté !
y vivre sans mélange :
mais l'espace n'est plus vacant
pour les oiseaux, les sirènes,
et l'on avance dans ce monde autre
où nul infini
n'équilibre
la dépossession.

Nous sommes entraînés dans une poursuite
qui se résout
dans l'accord tenu,
qui résonne en nous,
fend notre armature,

une fenêtre s'ouvre
sur le vent qui rôde
et parcourt la terre,

ANOTHER CITY

You are alone
in the city
with this threat
that the bird, from between your hands
takes flight,
and leaves you mute,
knowing only to watch
its flight.

Anxiety is still
behind the day rising…
O this clarity!
to live in it without mixture:
but the space is no longer vacant
for the birds, the sirens,
and someone moves closer in this other world
where no infinity
balances
dispossession.

We are led in a pursuit
that resolves
in the chord kept,
that echoes in us,
cracks our frame,

a window opens
to the wind that prowls
and covers the earth,

il va, il vient,
puis se révèle corrosif.
Le soir tombe.

> *On peut objecter que le ballet fantastique des jeux*
> *de lumière, leur réflexion dans les miroirs, les*
> *mouvements imprévus dans la transparence de la*
> *sculpture, atteindront leur maximum d'intensité*
> *pendant la nuit, aux heures où précisément le pouls*
> *de la ville baisse. N'y a-t-il pas là une contradiction*
> *? Je ne le pense pas, car de jour l'intensité des*
> *rayons solaires crée une luminosité différente mais*
> *aussi artistique que la nuit. Au sommet de la tour,*
> *un flash laser de dix mégawatts sera aussi visible à*
> *midi qu'à minuit.*

it goes, it comes,
then reveals itself corrosive.
Night falls.

> *One can object that the fantastic ballet of the games
> of light, its reflection in mirrors, the unexpected
> movements in the transparency of sculpture,
> achieves its maximum intensity during the night,
> at the hours precisely when the pulse of the city
> lowers. Is there not a contradiction here? I don't
> think so, because by day the intensity of the solar
> rays creates a different luminosity just as artistic
> as that of night. At the summit of the tower, a ten
> megawatt laser flash will be as visible at noon as
> at midnight.*

Trans. D. Jackson

JAZZ

*Et puis les projections en couleurs ne se perdent pas
dans l'atmosphère, elles plongent dans des miroirs
qui les répercutent. Aux moments de grande excitation,
des bombes à gaz fumigène exploseront, enveloppant
la tour de fumée. Alors seules les lumières émergeront,
scintillantes, ainsi que les lasers. Nous estimons que
l'ensemble cybernétique travaillera à raison de cinq
mille paramètres de fonction (moteurs, projecteurs,
flashes, lasers, etc.) et d'une cinquantaine de
paramètres d'information.*

Chant de cette jungle, qui s'intensifie ;
au delà des palissades,
les blocs du réel sont des masses obscurcies
entre lesquelles nous nous affairons,
nous suivons désormais la trajectoire des éléments,
observons, accompagnons de la voix ce qui est,
puissance des choses, tempérée par intervalles ;
au loin, le cor des pays enchantés se tait
et la dernière voix est humaine ;

un mouvement, une rumeur, cependant,
foules qui avancent,
obscurité qui gagne :
on ne sait pas encore,
les abords de la ville sont déserts,
personne ne semble entendre ou se préoccuper
de cette marée étrange,
elle approche, est-ce une tempête, est-ce une idée,
ou bien ce chant que nous rêvions ?

JAZZ

And since the color projections are not lost in
the atmosphere, they dive into mirrors that
reflect them. At moments of great excitation,
smoke bombs will explode, enveloping the
tower in smoke. So only the lights will emerge,
twinkling, as well as the lasers. We estimate
that the cybernetic ensemble will work using
some five thousand functional parameters
(motors, projectors, flashes, lasers, etc.) and
some fifty informational parameters.

Song of this jungle, deepening;
beyond the palisades,
the blocks of reality are obscured masses
between which we bustle about,
from now on we follow the trajectory of elements,
observe with our voice what is,
power of things, tempered by intervals;
far off, the horn of the enchanted countries quiets
and the last voice is human;

a movement, a rumor, however,
crowds advancing,
darkness gaining:
we still don't know,
the suburbs of the city are deserted,
nobody seems to hear or to be concerned
by this strange tide,
it approaches, is it a storm, an idea,
or just this song we dreamed?

Silence de l'attente,
les objets mouvants se fixent
dans la lumière qui se répand :
matin sur un quartier inconnu,
c'est la même ville, mais je ne la reconnais pas,
elle a des zones de poussière,
des rues larges où les marchés se montent ;
des gens un peu différents font des gestes
ordinaires,

on appelle, on parle du temps qu'il fait
et du ciel et des nuages qui y passent,
l'existence commune dans le frisson de froid
des premières heures ;
et, peu à peu, nous entrons dans cette journée,
ayant mesuré ce qui en fait la différence,
l'essai d'une nouvelle perception.

Silence of waiting,
moving objects are fixed
in spreading light:
morning in an unknown neighborhood,
it's the same city, but I don't recognize it,
it has zones of dust,
large streets where markets set up;
some people a little strange make ordinary
gestures,

someone calls out, someone talks of weather
and of the sky and clouds that pass there,
the common existence in the shivering cold
of the first hours;
and, little by little, we enter this day,
having measured what makes it different,
the attempt of a new perception.

Trans. D. Jackson

MURAILLES PIXELLISÉES

*Pour assurer la rentabilité de la tour, destinée à recevoir
plusieurs millions de visiteurs chaque année, les deux
tiers de la surface du socle seront loués ou vendus
à des exposants qui présenteront en permanence
l'échantillonnage complet de tous les objets et produits
se rapportant à l'environnement. En outre, il y aura une
plate-forme panoramique au sommet, et un restaurant
tournant (auquel on accédera du sol par ascenseur en
deux minutes), une salle de congrès pour sept cents
personnes, un jeu d'orgues manuel pour des concerts
où on pourra jouer sur les cinq mille paramètres de
la tour, etc.*

Récitatif devant le Palais,
tous deux parlent
devant ces murailles, ce matin ;
et son soleil peut sembler dissoudre la pierre,
comme, dans une peinture, pixellisés par l'intensité
érodante du soleil, les murs qui le réfractent.

Il les creuse et les vaporise,
ou bien, en les pointillisant,
les transmue en écrans mouvants,

— Quel essor pour la pensée ?

— Écoute l'air ductile,
scintillant d'étoffes,
ce dimanche, lorsque les groupes de femmes

PIXELATED WALLS

To assure the profitability of the tower, which is
destined to welcome millions of visitors each year,
two thirds of the base's surface will be rented or
sold to exhibitors who will permanently display a
comprehensive selection of environmental goods
and products. Moreover, there will be a viewing
platform at the top, a rotating restaurant (accessible
from the ground floor by means of a two-minute
elevator ride), an auditorium for seven hundred
people, a set of organ keyboards—used for
concerts—connected to the tower's five
thousand parameters, etc.

Recitative in front of the Palace,
both talking
in front of these walls this morning;
and its sun seems able to dissolve stone,
as, in a painting, pixelated by the sun's
eroding force, the walls that refract it.

It hollows them and vaporizes them,
or, while pointillizing them,
transmutes them into moving screens,

— How can thought take off?

— Listen to the ductile air,
sparkling with fabrics,
this Sunday, when groups

d'Afrique de l'Ouest
vont ainsi, dans les rues,
célébrant ce jour.

of West African women
stroll down the streets like this,
celebrating this day.

Trans. J.B. Anderson

NOTES

"Saint Sebastian." "Gaudier" is Henri Gaudier-Brzeska (1891–1915), the French sculptor born near Orléans who died in World War I. Known as a founder of Vorticism along with Wyndham Lewis and Ezra Pound.

"Strange Fruit" takes its title from the song about lynching made famous by Billie Holiday. Séville was the site of the military uprising that helped precipitate the Spanish Civil War.

"Ida, in the Mirror" is dedicated to Paul Bley (b. 1932), a Montreal-born jazz pianist.

"The Disenchanted City" memorializes a walk through London. "[T]he house / where everything had been said" is Sigmund Freud's final home, now the Freud Museum.

"Remembering Piero's Baptism." "Piero's Baptism" is Piero della Francesca's painting, *The Baptism of Christ*, currently in the National Gallery, London.

"Luxor, Movie Palace." The Luxor is a newly restored Egyptian Art Deco cinema in Paris. See introduction.

"Elssinore" is the name of Chantal's cat, who in turn was named for a character in Lautréamont's "Les chants de Maldoror."

"The Light Tower" is inspired by *Nun*, orchestral work by Helmut Lachenmann, with some phrases by painter-sculptor Nicolas Schöffer, referring to his architectural project, *Tour Lumière Cybernétique*.

CHANTAL BIZZINI is a poet, translator, photographer, and collage artist, who lives in Paris. She has published poetry and translations in *Po&sie, Europe, Poésie 2005, Action Poétique, Le Mâche-Laurier, Rehauts, Public Republic,* and *Siècle 21,* among other international literary journals. American poets she has translated extensively include Ezra Pound, Hart Crane, W. H. Auden, Adrienne Rich, Denise Levertov, John Ashbery, Clayton Eshleman, and Jorie Graham. Her own poetry has been translated into English, Italian, Spanish, and Greek. Her first volume of poetry, *Boulevard Magenta,* was published in 2015 by le bousquet-la barthe éditions.

Her current project involves a series of meditations on photo-illustrated books, including *The Bridge* by Hart Crane and Walker Evans; Rodenbach's *Bruges-la-Morte,* Brassaï's *Paris la nuit,* Walker Evans's *Many Are Called,* and Sebald's *Austerlitz.* She has lectured on this topic at the Sorbonne and New York University, among other venues.

MARILYN KALLET is the author or editor of
17 books including *The Love That Moves Me,* po-
etry, published by Black Widow Press. She has trans-
lated Paul Eluard's *Last Love Poems (Derniers
poèmes d'amour),* Benjamin Péret's *The Big Game
(Le grand jeu),* in addition to this new co-translation
with J. Bradford Anderson and Darren Jackson of
Chantal Bizzini's *Disenchanted City (La ville désenchantée).* Dr.
Kallet is Nancy Moore Goslee Professor of English at the Uni-
versity of Tennessee, Knoxville. She has performed her work on
campuses and in theaters across the United States, as well as in
Poland and in Auvillar, France, where she leads a poetry work-
shop each spring for VCCA-France.

J. BRADFORD ANDERSON is a teacher and
translator living in New York City. Anderson has
written on twentieth-century U.S. and Latin Ameri-
can Literature and was the lead translator of Alexan-
der von Humboldt's *Political Essay on the Island of
Cuba.* Anderson's translations of Chantal Bizzini's
poetry have appeared in the *Backwoods Broadsides*
series, *Two Lines: A Journal of Translation,* and *Esopus Maga-
zine.* He has been translating Bizzini for sixteen years. He is a
teacher of English and dean at Trinity School in Manhattan.

DARREN JACKSON's recent poems have ap-
peared in *The Pinch, The Laurel Review, The Of-
fending Adam, Bluestem,* and other journals. He has
also translated *Life in the Folds* by Henri Michaux
(Wakefield P, forthcoming Fall 2015); and "The
White Globe," an essay by Bertrand Westphal, which
is forthcoming from Northwestern University Press
in *The Planetary Turn: Art, Dialogue, and Geoaesthetics in the
21st-Century.* He holds a Ph.D. in English from the University of
Tennessee.

TITLES FROM BLACK WIDOW PRESS
TRANSLATION SERIES

A Life of Poems, Poems of a Life
by Anna de Noailles. Translated by Norman
R. Shapiro. Introduction by Catherine Perry.

Approximate Man and Other Writings
by Tristan Tzara. Translated and edited
by Mary Ann Caws.

Art Poétique by Guillevic.
Translated by Maureen Smith.

The Big Game by Benjamin Péret. Translated
with an introduction by Marilyn Kallet.

Boris Vian Invents Boris Vian:
A Boris Vian Reader.
Edited and translated by Julia Older.

Capital of Pain by Paul Eluard.
Translated by Mary Ann Caws,
Patricia Terry, and Nancy Kline.

Chanson Dada: Selected Poems by
Tristan Tzara. Translated with an
introduction and essay by Lee Harwood.

Essential Poems and Writings of
Joyce Mansour: A Bilingual Anthology.
Translated with an introduction
by Serge Gavronsky.

Essential Poems and Prose of Jules Laforgue.
Translated and edited by Patricia Terry.

Essential Poems and Writings of
Robert Desnos: A Bilingual Anthology.
Edited with an introduction and essay
by Mary Ann Caws.

EyeSeas (Les Ziaux) by Raymond Queneau.
Translated with an introduction by Daniela
Hurezanu and Stephen Kessler.

Fables in a Modern Key by Pierre Coran.
Edited and translated by Norman R. Shapiro.
Full-color illustrations by Olga Pastuchiv.

Forbidden Pleasures: New Selected Poems
[1924–1949] by Luis Cernuda.
Translated by Stephen Kessler.

Furor and Mystery & Other Writings
by René Char. Edited and translated
by Mary Ann Caws and Nancy Kline.

Guarding the Air:
Selected Poems of Gunnar Harding.
Translated and edited by Roger Greenwald.

The Inventor of Love & Other Writings
by Gherasim Luca. Translated by Julian &
Laura Semilian. Introduction by Andrei
Codrescu. Essay by Petre Răileanu.

Jules Supervielle: Selected Prose and Poetry.
Translated by Nancy Kline and Patricia Terry.

La Fontaine's Bawdy by Jean de La Fontaine.
Translated with an introduction by
Norman R. Shapiro.

Last Love Poems of Paul Eluard.
Translated with an introduction by
Marilyn Kallet.

Love, Poetry (L'amour la poésie)
by Paul Eluard. Translated with an essay
by Stuart Kendall.

Pierre Reverdy: Poems, Early to Late.
Translated by Mary Ann Caws and
Patricia Terry.

Poems of André Breton: A Bilingual Anthology.
Translated with essays by Jean-Pierre Cauvin
and Mary Ann Caws.

Poems of A.O. Barnabooth by Valery Larbaud.
Translated by Ron Padgett and Bill Zavatsky.

Poems of Consummation
by Vicente Aleixandre.
Translated by Stephen Kessler.

Préversities: A Jacques Prévert Sampler.
Translated and edited by Norman R. Shapiro.

The Sea and Other Poems
by Guillevic. Translated by Patricia Terry.
Introduction by Monique Chefdor.

To Speak, to Tell You? Poems by Sabine Sicaud.
Translated by Norman R. Shapiro. Intro-
duction and notes by Odile Ayral-Clause.

Forthcoming Translations

Earthlight (Clair de Terre)
by André Breton. Translated by Bill Zavatsky
and Zack Rogrow. (New and revised edition.)

The Gentle Genius of Cécile Périn:
Selected Poems (1906–1956).
Edited and translated by Norman R. Shapiro.

MODERN POETRY SERIES

ABC of Translation by Willis Barnstone

An Alchemist with One Eye on Fire
by Clayton Eshleman

Anticline by Clayton Eshleman

Archaic Design by Clayton Eshleman

Backscatter: New and Selected Poems
by John Olson

Barzakh (Poems 2000–2012) by Pierre Joris

The Caveat Onus by Dave Brinks

City Without People: The Katrina Poems
by Niyi Osundare

Concealments and Caprichos
by Jerome Rothenberg

Crusader-Woman by Ruxandra Cesereanu.
Translated by Adam J. Sorkin. Introduction
by Andrei Codrescu.

Curdled Skulls: Poems of Bernard Bador.
Translated by the author with
Clayton Eshleman.

Disenchanted City (La ville désenchantée)
by Chantal Bizzini. Edited by Marilyn Kallet
and J. Bradford Anderson. Translated by J.
Bradford Anderson, Darren Jackson, and
Marilyn Kallet.

Endure: Poems by Bei Dao. Translated by
Clayton Eshleman and Lucas Klein.

Exile Is My Trade: A Habib Tengour Reader.
Translated by Pierre Joris.

Eye of Witness: A Jerome Rothenberg Reader.
Edited with commentaries by Heriberto Yepez
& Jerome Rothenberg.

Fire Exit by Robert Kelly

Forgiven Submarine by Ruxandra Cesereanu
and Andrei Codrescu

from stone this running by Heller Levinson

The Grindstone of Rapport:
A Clayton Eshleman Reader

Larynx Galaxy by John Olson

The Love That Moves Me by Marilyn Kallet

Memory Wing by Bill Lavender

Packing Light: New and Selected Poems
by Marilyn Kallet

The Present Tense of the World: Poems
2000–2009 by Amina Saïd. Translated with
an introduction by Marilyn Hacker.

The Price of Experience by Clayton Eshleman

The Secret Brain: Selected Poems 1995–2012
by Dave Brinks

Signal from Draco: New and Selected Poems
by Mebane Robertson

Wrack Lariat by Heller Levinson

Forthcoming Modern Poetry Titles

An American Unconscious
by Mebane Robertson

Essential Poetry (1968–2015)
by Clayton Eshleman

Funny Way of Staying Alive
by Willis Barnstone

The Hexagon by Robert Kelly

Memory by Bernadette Mayer

Soraya (Sonnets) by Anis Shivani

LITERARY THEORY /
BIOGRAPHY SERIES

Barbaric Vast & Wild: A Gathering of Outside
and Subterranean Poetry (Poems for the
Millennium, v. 5) Eds: Jerome Rothenberg
and John Bloomberg-Rissman

Clayton Eshleman: The Whole Art
by Stuart Kendall

Revolution of the Mind:
The Life of André Breton
by Mark Polizzotti

WWW.BLACKWIDOWPRESS.COM